Alive to Change

Successful Museum Retailing

A Collection of Essays

MUSEUMSETC, EDINBURGH

Contents

1

Creating the Utopian Experience

GREGORY KRUM

Director of Retail

Cooper-Hewitt, National Design Museum

Smithsonian Institution

New York City

I started by imagining what was expected, then made sure I did something different. I began to see many possibilities to include work not usually represented in a museum shop. It became very personal. I expanded the price point to include limited edition and one-of-a-kind work and being the nation's design museum it really is an ideal place to see this kind of work. So much energy goes into making these special pieces: they need to be shown.

And, frankly, there was a gap in the market. I knew I had to differentiate this museum shop from all the others. There are so many great museum stores in New York that it's difficult to compete – especially with those that have ten times my resources! So it's really about using the intimate atmosphere to my advantage. We have personal control over each object that goes into the shop. This means I can act in a very agile way that some larger organizations cannot. I took a cue from the mansion's architecture and the upscale neighborhood to find what was possible.

That being said, I do want everyone to be able to participate; this is not a case for creating something prohibitive. The jewel-like element of the display cases focuses ones attention and elevates even humble objects. It's the spirit of the experience that goes home with the customer and even becomes a part of the object.

As far as the presentation of the products is concerned, it's mostly about respect. Respect for the museum, the customers, the building, the employees, the products we offer. I try to display the objects in the cleanest, simplest, most straightforward way I can. In most cases I know what it takes to just get these things produced - not only with the bespoke studio objects, but also the mass-manufactured. It takes an incredible amount of energy. A shop can be a wondrous, utopian experience. The display cases simply isolate the objects, light them well, so maybe you can see them in a different way.

In terms of the shop design, I thought it would be smart to build it out of existing, well-designed fixtures instead of trying to fake the *Belle Époque* architecture of the mansion or design something custom. I chose the Haller system designed in the early 1960s by Fritz Haller and made by the Swiss company USM. It is a classic icon of modern design. The lighting fixtures are designed by Konstantin Grcic for Flos - an important designer who makes super-smart objects. The USM system is exceptional in that it has a very bold structure but is very flexible. It's modular so has limitless possibilities. I was able to make the grids match the panelled walls and ceilings - the horizontal levels correspond exactly to the architectural details in the room. The overhead lights match the integrated lighting in the cases. I did challenge the system. I came up with configurations and uses that had never been done before - but they have a fantastic technical person who was able to make it all work. I felt the previous shop at the museum intervened a bit too much in the architecture. I thought it best to stimulate circulation by allowing people to walk around and through the cases. It is my tiny nod to I M Pei's entrance to the Louvre.

What challenges did we overcome? I'm sure all large institutions have a good deal of red tape but as the Smithsonian is a federal institution it proved to be doubly true. It was able to work, however, through the great support of the director and the board. They trusted in the project enough to give it freedom.

My advice to others: be specific, be bold and be practical! Amplify the idiosyncrasies. Above all, keep it clean!

How do we go about sourcing products? We're lucky because design and commerce have always gone hand-in-hand. Of course all art is sold, but in a more complicated and secret way. The museum has a wonderful collection and I'm constantly combing the world for objects or designers that are in the collection and that are also being produced. I really prefer not to reproduce objects at this point, if only because there is already so much great work already being done. I find most of the objects by attending major European trade shows: *Maison et Objet* in Paris, *Ambiente* in Frankfurt and *Salone del Mobile* in Milan. Lately, however, I've been working directly with designers to create something specific for the shop, or small production objects made in their studio – objects that never see the huge trade fairs. This is very exciting.

Buying the books for the shop is one of the great pleasures of my job! When I started I knew nothing about buying books. I went to every publisher of architecture, design, jewellery, graphics, and figurative arts books to actually look at the books themselves and to go through all the backlist titles. I'm happy to say that books account for almost half of the sales. There is no way I can compete with online booksellers, so the books I offer are a super-specialized selection. Many are obscure, hard- to-find, or imported titles – many not available on the large online booksellers or through the standard book wholesalers.

I'm not really a marketing person. I try not to imagine what the customer wants. I cover the categories I can with the best products based on my experience and everything I have seen. I do believe if you do something well and passionately, people will want to be a part of it. Obviously we have a locked-in audience interested, on whatever level, in design. Our museum is one where if you are there you are probably there on purpose – meaning not a general tourist on a circuit of the regular cultural sites. Had that been the case, the product selection would certainly be different.

But museum shops are different from other stores. People do not show up with a list of necessities. They are in the museum to learn – and the shop should be a part of that. Mainly, I try not to speak down to the customers – meaning that everything in there is a great example of whatever it is. The selection has to be able to speak to a casual visitor as well as impress the most informed professional.

Having an expert knowledge of the museum's collection is essential. The shop should be an interesting and dynamic extension of the museum and, of course, particular to that museum. There is a captive audience already present wanting to learn. Commerce is another way for them to participate. And it makes perfect sense for the product to relate to the museum in the most specific way possible. I turn down great product all the time that doesn't relate to our museum – it is a boundary to focus the shop's collection. The collection is what makes the museum unique. We've all seen too much of the same.

I love walking into other shops that are so deep in

one subject, so specific, so beyond my knowledge of a given topic. I can spend hours in them – and usually come out with something totally unexpected.

How do we ensure we provide the best financial return to the museum while still upholding the institution's high standards? Well, my mother worked creatively in the graphic arts and my father was an engineer. So I constantly have these two opposing forces checking themselves. For me, each problem is approached simultaneously from these two points of view.

I'm aware of what sells and what doesn't sell and the good selling locations in the store. But I'll still keep something truly wonderful in the shop even if it doesn't sell. The wonder of one thing sells another. If someone can't participate at a high price point, it's the surprise and joy of seeing those products that I hope would lead them to buy a more modest product. I always make sure that after seeing all these amazing objects in the museum and in the shop if you leave with a $20 pen at least you know it's going to be a good one!

I know that the shop must make money. If it didn't no one would speak to me. I enjoy the challenge. We buy in a very specific way that allows almost no waste and very little risk. Almost everything sells and we rarely have to discount anything. It's very time consuming but it works.

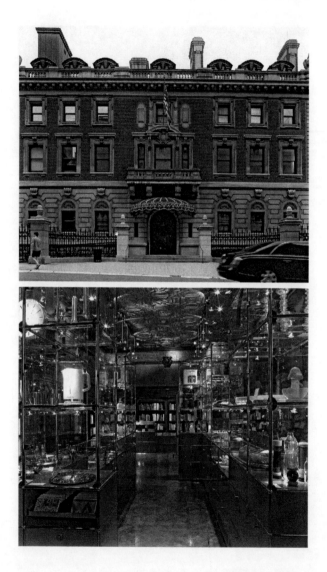

MORE IMAGES: WWW.MUSEUMSETC.COM/?PAGE _ ID=1378

MORE IMAGES: WWW.MUSEUMSETC.COM/?PAGE _ ID=1378

MORE IMAGES: WWW.MUSEUMSETC.COM/?PAGE_ID=1378

2

Children in Shops

LOUISA ADKINS

Retail Manager, Compton Verney

Children are important in the heritage retail environment not only as buyers, but also as influencers. At Compton Verney, we aim to have children's products represented across all the ranges in our shop, as well as the traditional branded souvenir items that will appeal to the child on an outing.

The primary purchase power of children is when they attend as part of a school group; here they can buy any completely impractical and much repeated item without the interference of the adult in their life. In our first season at Compton Verney we produced a branded range in our brand palette colours of blues, greens and browns which represent the landscape. Unfortunately it wasn't a big hit with our discerning younger visitors, so we added a purple line and a bit of glitter and sales grew. This was a bit of a compromise, but the products still bear our logo and the children enjoy them more, which seems reasonable.

We are trying to develop a range of goodie bags at the moment to offer an alternative to the *en masse* shopping experience. Our rural location means some school groups have quite a journey to get here, making schedules tight, so it is easier for them to collect a box of pre-prepared best-sellers rather than rush each child through the shop. It is also offers the teachers a less stressful experience, although as a bit of a shopaholic

I think it is a shame for the children!

The secondary purchase power of children revolves around the family visit. Here we have less success with the branded merchandise so we ensure that there are reasonably-priced toys in our other ranges. Our folk art range offers particular scope for this where we sell traditional wooden toys. We also offer a range of creative play products, which sell well, particularly around school holidays, offering an alternative to the digital age appreciated by many.

Children's books are also a particularly big market for us. On one of our first trading days a family with four children came into the shop and the mother rejected everything they asked for over £1 until one of the children showed her a book which she allowed him to have immediately, saying to me, "I never refuse if they actually show an interest in books!" I took this on board and it does seem to be reflected in the shop where one of our best selling items is the Doodle Book at £9.99. This is a price point I believe most parents would be unwilling to spend on many other items children ask for!

Children's products offer an injection of fun into heritage shops which I think can sometimes be missing. They also allow you to make good margins. It is interesting that we bought in animals that stick their tongues out as part of the children's offer in our out-door range and nearly as many of these, if not more, go back on the coaches of our more senior customers than our most junior!

3

Making a Success of Online Retailing

KATE BULL

Director, CTWB Ltd

During December 2008 alone, online shopping exceeded all expectations. According to the IMRG index, a massive £4.67 billion was spent online by British consumers in the run up to Christmas. This is the equivalent of three out of five gifts being bought over the Internet or around £4 in every £10 spent. The growth of e-retailing, not just at Christmas, seems to know no bounds – online sales for the whole of 2008 came to over £65 billion.

But what does this trend towards online shopping mean for the heritage and museum sector? Is it a not-to-be-missed retail opportunity offering the chance to increase revenues? Or is it a step too far, particularly for the smaller, independent museums and heritage attractions?

For many museums and heritage attractions it is indeed an opportunity to be exploited. We are increasingly seeing more and more examples of good online shops from this sector, and they are sure to be reaping the benefits. The Victoria and Albert Museum's online shop (www.vandashop.com) is a shining example of a good e-retailing outlet. It is beautifully laid out; its products are fantastic and in harmony with the V&A's core values. It is easy to find what you are looking for or just to browse, and – perhaps most importantly – it's easy to purchase the goods.

Aside from potentially increasing revenue, there are

other benefits to consider, such as meeting customer expectations. Do your customers expect an online shop? For most of the bigger museums and heritage attractions, if they don't today, they almost certainly will do tomorrow. Moreover, e-retailing increases the number of customers you can reach. The potential market is huge – worldwide even! And finally, the Internet is another way of marketing the museum or attraction. It provides a further opportunity to promote your branding, offerings and core values.

For some of the smaller heritage attractions, having a web presence that provides the basic information about what's on, opening hours, directions, what's new or coming up, is more than enough. The business case for an online shop needs to be robust. According to the Office of Fair Trading, most non-financial Internet traders in the UK make less than £15,000 per year. Take from that the significant resources (people and finances) required for set-up, maintenance and fulfilment and it might not be the pot of gold you envisaged. Worse still, a badly managed online shop can be damaging to the organisation's reputation, in the same way that a badly managed retail outlet can be. So think hard before you embark on this journey.

If this is a route you want to go down, then there are five areas to consider:

- what your online shop will look like;
- what it will sell;
- how to meet customer needs;
- how to market the online shop;
- how to evaluate its success.

The look

Rather like creating the ambience of your shop, the web designer will create a virtual look and feel. It often helps to provide the designer with examples of websites you do and don't like. Don't be bamboozled or scared by the technical language, you just need to provide a clear brief as you would a shopfitter or architect.

The main thing to concentrate on is ease of use and accessibility. The Tate (www.tate.org.uk/shop), for example, divides its products into five simple categories: gift ideas, books, prints and cards, exhibitions, and artists' products. It also has space for an extra category that it can change, for example when it wants to highlight sale items. When considering ease of use and accessibility make sure you look at: use of colours and inclusion of your branding, font type and size (especially relevant for people with limited vision), number of pages, how products are categorised, methods of payment, terms and conditions, and how easy it will be for you to update the website with new products.

Finally, make sure your web designer tests the site on different size screens and web browsers to make sure it looks good and works well on the majority of computers.

The content

The next step is to consider what you are going to sell online. You don't have to put your entire product range online – in fact it is often a good idea to limit the choice according to your key strengths. A good example of an organisation that has thought this through is Wookey Hole Caves. Aside from the caves, Wookey Hole is famous for owning Britain's last surviving handmade paper mill. Rather than put all the products from its shop online, it has just chosen to sell its handmade paper online (www.wookey.co.uk/papermill.htm). For them, I imagine this is a manageable solution and it builds on its unique selling proposition (or USP to use marketing speak).

The simplest retail web packages hold up to 12 photographs and descriptions per page. Until you have collected accurate web sales data, this is a reasonable size range to start with. Continuing with the store analogy, these photographs and product descriptions represent not only your shop window, but also your point of sale *décor*. So it is really important that they are of a high quality resolution and you might even consider taking a variety of shots to highlight the details. The pictures should have a consistent look and feel - they should all be taken in the same light and with the same background. The accompanying descriptions should reflect the tone of voice used through out the site. You can always break down the descriptions, so that the catchy selling features are immediately visible and then more detailed specifications are accessible through a link.

One of the trickiest aspects is working out how to charge for postage and packaging. Remember that often as much work goes into sending a £1 item as a £10 item. Most sites offer a flat rate to the UK and Ireland for the whole order, no matter how many items; others vary it according to the weight of the items, the number of items, or the amount spent. Whichever route you take, make sure you do a "sense check" on the final price the purchaser will pay on each item ensuring that it still seems reasonable.

Meeting customers' needs

All retailers want to offer excellent customer service and operating through the web should be no different. However, it is more complicated as the relationship is a virtual one. Bear in mind that your customer's journey starts at the home page and carries on right through to delivery of the product, so you need to ensure that, - all the way through this journey - you are delivering to the highest standards, from the layout of the web pages to the wrapping and paperwork. Establish from the outset your own internal standards. For example, what will the turnaround time be for orders - 24 hours or two working days? How will customers receive the products – sturdy boxes, attractive wrapping and clear paperwork? All these things will add to the customer's perception of the quality of service they have received.

It is always worthwhile establishing whose responsibility it is to ensure that orders are dealt with and customer queries are answered. It is surprising how time-consuming these things can be, as anyone who has ever sold anything on eBay will tell you.

Marketing an online shop

Opening an e-shop shifts your business from being part of a heritage site or museum to being a standalone store which, for many, has the added advantage of freeing it from curatorial constraints. Subsequently, it deserves its own marketing, bearing in mind what works in the real world may not translate to the virtual world.

The best way to market your website is to have it

listed on the major search engines such as Google, Yahoo or MSN. Each website must have key words or phrases attached to it (which aren't usually visible). So, for example, an art gallery's keywords might include: art, gallery, free, Sundays, families, fairtrade, London, contemporary, urban, shop, prints, frames, etc. Remember to include any specialist items or unique collections to help you reach a worldwide audience for them.

Getting listed on search engines is free, but your place on the page is usually dependent on the popularity of your site or the precision of the research request. Fine if you are the British Library, but not so good if you are smaller institution. If you type *library* into Google, then British Library will come out at the top of the list; or type *British* and it comes out in third position – not bad! For the rest of us smaller players, paying is the only answer. Google Advertising is easy to use. A link to your website is listed in a separate column on the right hand side and you pay for each click through to your site. You can cap the number of clicks per month so it is possible to control your advertising spend.

One of the beauties of the Internet is the ability to link between compatible sites. This is often a reciprocal and free-of-charge agreement where you link to their website and they link to yours. Consider which sites might be most appropriate. Look at local tourist boards for example, interest groups related to your collections (don't forget to think global), local newspapers, accommodation sites, etc. The Motor Boat Museum does this well – go to www.motorboatmuseum.org.uk and click on the *links* tab in the top right hand corner.

Evaluating success

Obviously there are the sales that your e-shop generates, but that is not the be-all-and-end-all of evaluation. Don't forget the softer benefits of being online, such as raising the awareness and appreciation of your museum or attraction, reinforcing your core values, reducing the volume of mundane enquiries because the information can found online, and so on. One way to evaluate some of these aspects is to look at your viewing figures. Most web hosting companies can provide you with data on the number of hits per page and how long viewers stayed on each page. You can gain a better understanding of your customers' profile by collecting data through your site, but you must make sure you have a good understanding of the current Data Protection Laws. Collate as much information as you can and use it to improve the site. For example, which items sell well? Which pages are the most popular? How often do people get part way through a sale and stop? What is causing this?

Consumers are turning to the Internet in their droves; not only for information, but increasingly to do their shopping. Putting your retail outlet online provides an excellent opportunity to promote your museum or attraction, reinforce the brand and create a whole new source of revenue. It is, however, a major undertaking that needs careful thought. If I was restricted to just one piece of advice for retailers going online for the first time, then I'd say: "Do it in small steps, but make each step brilliant."

ALIVE TO CHANGE

Designers at Tate

Tate works with selected designers to create unique gift ideas.

Ally Capellino Range >

Alice Melvin >   **Sara Fanelli** >   **Curwen Press** >   **Mimi** >

Melvin Owl Bag £9.79
£9.79

Tate Artist Timeline
£7.34

Curwen Pattern Paper
Book Bag
£8.32

Mimi Leather Grey
Green Bag
£112.55

MORE IMAGES: WWW.MUSEUMSETC.COM/?PAGE _ ID=1378

orderline +44 (0)20 7942 2696
The V&A Shop currently sends all orders
by courier services at no extra cost

Christmas
at the V&A Shop
Free P&P when you spend £50 and over

UK delivery only - Offer ends 30th November

Sign up for e-newsletter | Enter your email address | ▶ |

Every purchase supports the
Victoria and Albert Museum

CONTACT US | L

Home > Books & Media > New & Future Books > Medieval and Re...

Mec
(Boc
By G

Onli

Publ

This
V&A
them
mus
to re

Rath
Med
this I
that
often
intro
chap
clas:
whic

DIME
287 :

| Enter keyword to search | ▶ |

Shop by product

Books & Media
Book of the Month
New & Future Books
Exhibition Books   +
All Books - By Subject   +
V&A Publishing   +
Media

P&P

4

Selling Warhol:
Embracing the Commercial

ADAM THOW

Head of Retail Buying

Southbank Centre, London

"A dream exhibition for the commercial team" was how the news that we were to host a major Warhol show at the Hayward Gallery was met.

It was true in more ways than one. Not only did it mean that we could be brazenly commercial with the tacit approval of the curatorial team, it also meant that we had a diverse and expansive range of licensed goods to choose from.

The initial blessing also presented a challenge, mostly to our perceptions of what the gallery's shop is and what it should sell.

This was predicated on the sheer scope of what could be done in relation to Warhol: the licensed goods encompassed everything from fragrance, jeans, dresses, vases, skateboards and watches to the more usual stationery, magnets, diaries and mugs.

When faced with such mainstream retail product, one was forced to appraise what was possible within the store, to question what people would expect to see and what price points we could realistically expect to stretch to.

Would your average gallery attendee expect to see a £140 dress in what was previously, albeit erroneously, considered a bookshop?

The first consideration was why not? And if not then wouldn't it be interesting and ultimately fruitful to confound expectations, to change ingrained perceptions of what cultural sector retailing was?

Museum and heritage retail has gone through sea changes in recent years in the UK, to the extent that the majority of the large galleries have caught up with our US cousins in offering a 21st century retail experience. The latter is the operative word: there needs to be theatre, a high standard of visual presentation and imagination in product range, as consumers expect the retail experience to reflect - possibly even excel - the standards of their cultural experience.

The only limitations to experiment in the store are the fabric of the space and the financial risk that you may place the institution at. The latter we managed to mitigate to a large extent through negotiations with the majority of the suppliers. The former we managed to address through similar means.

Once the suppliers were approached they were keen to be associated not only with the show but also with the gallery itself. It gives added kudos to a brand to be associated with an educational, cultural or heritage organisation, not only because of the credibility by association, but also because they can generally guarantee a footfall that not all retail spaces can.

This can be used as leverage when it comes to negotiations. If the supplier cannot help with the price points they almost certainly can help with point-of-sale materials, display, mannequins, uniforms, training or PR. All of this was hugely beneficial in being able to adapt what for us was a very restrictive and conservative space into something more visually arresting and in the spirit of the exhibition.

There was more or less no budget for shop redesign for the exhibition. However, we were furnished with amazing props and mannequins from Pepe Jeans London, a major Warhol licensee. They supplied premium quality silver mannequins, giant soup cans and oversized Brillo boxes that complimented the product and set the tone for the theme of the shop.

What they supplied was worth several thousand Euros and, crucially, was Warhol Foundation approved. It had been used in flagship Pepe retail units, top London department stores and in fashion shoots and product launches throughout Europe.

Through working with our Development Department, the supplier also furnished us with props for the opening night party, dressing staff in their clothing and helping to create a sense of theatre for the occasion.

Other suppliers also rose to the occasion with a print-on-demand unit coming with a Campbell's soup can wrap, giant *Marilyn* prints for behind our till points and high quality stands for some of the key publications.

We worked with our commercial partner, MDC, to supply Warhol-related music to lift the atmosphere, giving them a credit at the till point in return.

The remainder of the shop props carried through themes from the exhibition and complemented the supplier's props. These were not expensive, purchased from the stalwart of inexpensive props, DZD, but displayed imaginatively to give height to the table pieces and to emphasise desired routes around the store.

We sought further assistance from the manufacturers in the shape of visual merchandising help to ensure that the product was displayed prominently and professionally, particularly in the key area opposite the exit from the exhibition.

In addition to this we employed the services of a consultant visual merchandiser for a few days, a worthwhile investment to create theatre and ensure strong displays were deployed from the beginning of the exhibition.

With regard to the merchandise, the more unusual offerings - perfume in an art gallery anyone? - were the ones that the press got excited about with major national newspapers and magazines doing features on the product and the exhibition.

We are not yet blessed with an online shop, so the benefit to sales cannot truly be measured, but as an exercise in shifting preconceptions and positioning the shop as a venue in its own right it was advertising that could not have been bought.

For maximum exposure of the Warhol range we offered taster ranges in our other retail units and turned one of our most prominent window displays over to Warhol.

The bold display, again supported by a supplier, in an area of maximum footfall ensured that a clientele, which may not have been exposed to the exhibition, let alone the shop, was made aware of the range.

Whilst the range was expansive and diverse, we didn't abandon traditional merchandise - there is a reason that it has been around so long and that is because generally it works.

We were also mindful of accessibility with regards to pricing and so ensured that there was still plenty of choice for £5 and under and £10 and under. Whilst our driving focus was not on making sure we could sell as many 60p postcards as possible, it was still an integral element of the range planning.

We were also mindful that high ticket lines tend to not to give you optimum margin and so a fine balancing act was walked, with the purchase of bespoke, high volume, high margin lines that fitted the look and feel of the exhibition and that didn't jar with the premium lines. These tended to be thematic, colour and icon-led to match the overall palette but not branded as such so that no royalty payments, with the entire administrative burden that they imply, were due.

Books were still an integral part of the plan also but only those publishers who gave the desired margins were given face-outs, prominent positions or table stacks to minimise the downward drag on margin.

The actions we applied during *Warhol* could not, of course, be applied to just any exhibition that happens at the Hayward Gallery. Being such an icon of popular, commercial art *Warhol* was the perfect vehicle through which to reposition the shop.

It does, however, give us the perfect springboard to move forward for future exhibitions, giving us tangible evidence of price point barriers, good knowledge of the restrictions of our shop layout and an invigorated confidence to innovate in the future.

It also points towards a more streamlined book offer, really targeting the key themes and supporting publishers who offer support back.

Already in planning upcoming exhibitions, where we may have been cautious in applying anything other than postcard/notebook/mug thinking, we are experimenting with theme and form, colour, texture and moods to create ranges that may surprise the guest but still feel like a natural progression from the gallery space.

The biggest growth areas for us from the past few exhibitions, even prior to *Warhol*, were jewellery and homeware. These are not areas traditionally associated with art gallery retail spaces but the sales figures indicate that if they are presented with relevance to the artistic programme that the guest is willing to purchase.

Given the pressures on heritage and art gallery commercial spaces to produce as much revenue as possible it is obviously in their interest to maximise sales per square foot and increase average transaction values. Even in times of economic uncertainty, homeware is an area that tends to remain fairly impervious to tightened spending as homeowners look to make quick "nest feathering" gains rather than large purchases.

Homeware also looks great in-store, is easy to display and creates strong centrepieces around which to position ranges.

The commerciality of the *Warhol* exhibition and product range inspired a rethink about what our gallery shop could be. It pointed to the fact that we can offer a lifestyle experience shop, mirroring colours, themes and images from the exhibition space but still with a strong academic backbone and with credibility intact. It raised the bar for us in terms of visuals and theatre and in collaborating with suppliers. It also gave us more confidence in being unapologetically commercial, for as Warhol himself once said, "Being good in business is the most fascinating kind of art. Making money is art..."

MORE IMAGES: WWW.MUSEUMSETC.COM/?PAGE _ ID=1378

MORE IMAGES: WWW.MUSEUMSETC.COM/?PAGE_ID=1378

5

Towards a More Environmentally Focused Future

CAROLINE BROWN

Head of Commerce

National Maritime Museum

As retailers in heritage and cultural institutions we are facing the same environmental realities as all other businesses and I believe it is time to reflect on the seriousness of the situation and look towards making changes for our future. This is not comfortable or easy and few of us can claim expertise in the wake of mind-boggling and often highly technical information or complex carbon trading schemes.

So what are the environmental challenges facing us, and how as small retailers in a unique market should we respond? As food retailing amounts to 85% of the UK retail market is it really a challenge worth approaching by museum and heritage retailers at all? And if the problem is real enough to demand change how we can respond whilst maintaining profitable sales?

Recently, The United Nations Environment Programme (UNEP) announced that the breakaway of a Jamaica-sized ice shelf from the Antarctic Peninsula could accelerate global warming in this already vulnerable region. Satellite pictures show a 40-kilometre ice bridge that was the Wilkins Ice Shelf's last link to the coast had now shattered at its narrowest point.

Against such a dramatic backdrop we could, of course, see our small efforts as practically useless. But there are those that see our current difficulties as an opportunity for re-evaluation and change. A recent commentary in *The Observer* newspaper ran "Let's see Climate Change as an Opportunity" and went on:

"If we continue to pollute the planet at our current rate, terrible consequences will follow. The evidence is there. But our leaders cannot find the will to do anything about it.

"Even by the standards of international diplomacy this is slow progress. It makes a sorry comparison with the urgency that world leaders have summoned in response to global financial meltdown and with the vast sums of money that were quickly pledged to bail out broken banks and car industries. The threat of climate meltdown and broken eco systems is by any measure greater. Who will bail out the planet?

"The financial crisis has shattered the free market orthodoxy that drove policy for a generation. We can now develop a new political philosophy, one that has the principles of environmental sustainability at its core - that presents the threat of climate change not as inevitable apocalypse, but as an opportunity.

"There is an antidote to climate defeatism: it is the knowledge that actions we take now to lead a greener life could boost employment and develop an economy less dependent on wasteful financial services, improve national security by making us less dependent on fossil fuels, and deliver us a better, healthier, happier lifestyle. It so happens they will also preserve the planet for future generations."

Far from deterring us from making changes, could the current financial slowdown force us to re-evaluate our core values and our commercial approaches? In reality we can no longer escape having to face up to an increasing problem in our environment and we cannot remain innocent or naïve to the impacts that we as retailers have upon the world around us.

However, even the most successful museum and heritage trading companies in the UK are, in reality, relatively small businesses and it may be the sheer scale of the problem that we are confronted with, along with a lack of clear information for smaller scale retailers, that is hindering our approaches to dealing with the problem.

I believe that the current challenges should enable us to refocus our efforts and that as companies within the cultural sector we are uniquely placed to engage with innovative designers and suppliers and to lead instead of follow when it comes to environmentally friendlier and sustainable retailing. We can certainly ride on the coat tails of the massive shift in response from food retailers and an increasing number of High Street clothing companies, but due to our scope and scale we need to do this in an innovative and smaller way.

If we do not change, I believe we will find ourselves adrift, without a sustainable future, not only ignoring our impact on the planet, but also increasingly out of step with policy makers and the views of a younger and increasingly aware generation – our future customers.

Although the media increasingly represents young people as narcissicistic and disengaged from the world around them, we need to acknowledge that some of them are increasingly participating in political activity, such as the recent and largely non-violent G20 protests and joining groups such as *Plane Stupid* and the *Climate Change Camp*. People's awareness and values are shifting – take a walk down any UK High Street and count the number of *Bags for Life* in use – this may seem like tokenism but I believe we are seeing the signs of a seismic shift which we would do well to watch.

There are calls for governments to fundamentally change their approaches to finance and climate change and to take radical steps to work together towards meaningful change. As the US Government finally acknowledged the dangers of CO_2 emissions, others have gone much further: Mohammed Nasheed, President of the Republic of Maldives recently announced that the Maldives will become the world's first carbon neutral country, and was quoted as saying:

"Last week experts meeting in Copenhagen reported dangerous new cracks in polar ice that could lead to dramatic sea-level rises. Scientists also cautioned that unless the world wakes up to climate warming, 85% of the Amazon rainforest could die.

"People often tell me caring for the environment is too difficult, too expensive or too much bother. I admit installing solar panels and wind turbines doesn't come cheap; but when I read those science reports from Copenhagen, I know there is only one choice. Going green might cost a lot but refusing to act now will cost us the earth."

As retailers in a new era of frugality we need to source products which reflect a new interest in local, authentic and ethical products and which have function, meaning or intrinsic design value.

There is an increased interest in activities such as cooking, sewing and growing your own vegetables as people reflect on the ethical and financial costs of a throwaway society. B&Q recently reported a threefold increase in the sale of chicken coops as people seek closer engagement with nature and food production. This is not just a frugality borne of a lack of cash; it is one of nostalgia for a simpler, more honest age which we mythically believe existed somewhere in our recent past. Whatever the legitimacy of the image, it may be true to say that anyone ignoring these underlying trends will quickly become irrelevant in an increasingly aware market place.

However, we live in a confusing world where newspapers feature articles on imminent climate disaster alongside adverts for £5 flights, and as consumers we are torn about our priorities. Perhaps as retailers we have a responsibility to ensure that some of those choices are easier and clearer for our customers.

In short, are we doing enough in our sector? Are we innovators or are we are in danger of falling behind the general trends on the High Street? We are well aware that retail within museums and heritage institutions often falls behind the parent institution in terms of investment and focus and there is a danger that we also fall behind in our approaches to the environment, as it is safer to stay within the known parameters of traditional heritage retailing rather than embrace significant and painful change.

Of course, there have been changes and I suspect most of us now stock some form of recycled bag or *Bag for Life*, and use environmentally friendly packaging. It is also true to say that some institutions stock eco-products and it is no surprise that these are more apparent in shops in science or environmentally-focused institutions such as the Natural History Museum, the Science Museum or the National Trust. There have also been major initiatives such as the Fair Trade shops at both the Manchester and Liverpool Museums - but where does that leave the rest of us?

Despite scouring the online shops of many heritage and museum retailers I found no policy statements regarding environmental policies, even when these were clearly stated in the mission statement of the parent institution.

Of course the National Maritime Museum is no exception and we need to work hard towards achieving the standards and ambitions set by the wider museum. Indeed it is the museum's commitment to sustainability that has led me increasingly to question our commercial approaches and to believe that small steps can lead to significant changes.

Part of the National Maritime Museum's policy regarding sustainability states:

The Museum recognises its sustainability obligations to its staff, visitors, communities and stakeholders – both locally and globally – and to present and succeeding generations.

The Museum aims to take a leading role in defining best sustainability practice, and will set its own appropriate and demanding standards where none exist.

And it continues: *The Sustainability Policy of the National Maritime Museum will be applicable to all its activities and across all its sites.*

So, how can we as retailers keep in step with our overarching ambitions and remain in line with the policies of our parent institutions?

Again, choices are difficult, as even many recycled products do not provide any easy solution to our stock procurement issues. Many of them are produced in China and shipped to the UK, and we cannot simply ignore the climate impact of the shipping industry or the fact that goods manufactured in China tend to have a larger carbon imprint than those manufactured here in the UK.

Ultimately, we all need help and support as few of us are experts, and wading through Government publications such as the Stern Report can be difficult and in the end too large-scale to be relevant to a small retailer.

So where can we get help and what steps can we take?

The British Retail Consortium recognises the difficulty for the smaller retailer in their report *Towards Retail Sustainability*, but equally puts some responsibilities squarely on our own shoulders.

The report "recognises that smaller retailers do not

necessarily have the resources or the market influence to monitor their suppliers but must rely on the influence of larger retailers, wholesalers' international standards and verification schemes.

"Large retailers tend to have the resources and infrastructure in place to focus on up-and-coming issues and use any influencing power that they have to tread a path for others to follow at their pace. Smaller independent retailers generally have less control. All retailers are part of the supply chain and all of them have a part to play as do suppliers, manufacturers, distributors, the government, consumers and the media. Retailers can and should do their bit as part of the supply chain team to control their operations and facilitate change elsewhere by encouraging suppliers to develop their practices and by educating consumers to the choices open to them."

There is useful information, too, from research conducted by some of the UK's leading ethical businesses: the *Ethical Consumerism Report* from 2008 by the Co-operative Bank for instance is a succinct and useful document which can help inform our decision making processes as smaller retailers:

"As the UK economy enters an economic downturn, many commentators are predicting that consumers will switch their priority from *values* to *Value*, bringing an end to the growth that has been seen in ethical markets over the last five to six years. Of course, ethical markets remain small and vulnerable. However, this Report shows that despite the first tremors of the downturn being felt towards the end of last year, overall ethical spend in the UK reached £35.5 billion in 2007, up 15% from £31 billion in the previous 12 months. It would appear that green legislation and choice editing are playing a significant role in maintaining momentum in the ethical markets... We are now seeing that Government intervention, which promotes energy efficient products such as boilers, white goods and more recently light bulbs, is underpinning these markets and ensuring that they continue to grow. In addition, consumers' emotional attachment to many ethical products is now well embedded, and we would argue that these areas will have an advantage over other markets in a downturn, particularly where the premium for the ethical choice is relatively low, as with Fairtrade. In addition, some ethical choices appeal to consumers' economic sensibilities as much as to their emotions, and energy saving products with an economic payback would appear well-placed to deal with the economic climate.

"Of course, the state of the economy will impact on consumer spending and on ethical markets. However,

SUCCESSFUL MUSEUM RETAILING

we would argue that Government intervention to
stimulate these markets and further choice editing
will ensure that the economic downturn will not stop
the growth of ethical consumerism."

Of course, in reality it is the food sector which leads
on environmental awareness in retailing and it is the
large retail players who have delivered most in terms
of the public perception of the impact of retail on the
environment, food miles, packaging and sustainable
sourcing.

All the major food retailers have written statements
and targets and there is no doubt that their policies
are having an impact on our day-to-day behaviour. I
doubt that any of them would claim perfection, but it
is clear that they see value (both in terms of money and
reputation) in wearing their green credentials on their
sleeves: whether it is M&S's *Plan A* scheme emblazoned
on every bag and sandwich wrapper, or supermarkets
setting off style wars such as the *I am not a plastic bag*
initiative.

Both Sainsbury's and Asda have opened Eco stores
recently, ensuring both significant press copy and
a tangible statement about their Eco philosophy.
According to the press statement released by
Sainsbury's: "The pioneering store will save 40% of its
overall CO_2 emissions... Using no gas whatsoever at the

store, this system uses renewable energy and means energy currently taken from the national grid will now be slashed by 50%. Rainwater will be collected, and used to flush customer and colleague toilets, and to irrigate plants... The store will save over one million litres of mains water every year, and uses 60% less water overall. Lower lighting levels, the use of daylight and dimming light also make carbon savings, and cool air will be collected from chillers to keep the store cool during warmer months. Plus the lights at the back area of the store turn off if no-one's there. The store's construction is also environmentally responsible, and where possible recycled or recyclable materials have been used or FSC-approved timber. As 200 trees have been used for the frame of the store, Sainsbury's will also re-plant 400 trees in the local community."

Sainsbury's now plans to replicate many of the sustainable features of the Dartmouth store across the UK, and pledges to open a minimum of two green supermarket-sized stores every year, plus a greener Sainsbury's Local, as well as extending existing stores with a range of environmental measures.

Supermarkets are not alone in trumpeting their ethical values – clothes stores are on the case with major High Street players such as H&M making commitments towards the use of organic cotton.

According to their website, H&M wants to actively contribute to reducing the environmental impact of cotton growing: "Our intention is to gradually use more cotton that has been grown organically – that is without the use of chemical pesticides or synthetic fertilizers. We want to contribute towards increased demand and thereby motivate more growers to invest in organic cotton growing. During 2008 we expect to use around 3,000 tonnes of organic cotton – a marked increase from the 30 tonnes used in 2006."

Of course, these are big players and it is unlikely that we can have such dramatic changes in the short term in our own organisations; however it does indicate that these policies matter to the retailers and therefore ultimately to the consumer, and as the big retailers no doubt have an impact on consumer behaviour, we cannot afford to fall too far behind.

I think we would do well to set our own achievable, if stretching, targets and perhaps the smaller and quirkier Howies clothing company might give us some food for thought with their slightly off-beat approach. I will quote three of their beliefs which I think can give us all some inspiration:

"Our beliefs: A higher quality product will invariably last longer. It will keep on performing as it was designed to for longer before it finally

needs replacing. And so over its lifespan it will have consumed less valuable resources than an inferior product that will have been replaced many times...

"We believe in making products that serve a purpose and that stand the test of time. We avoid the fashions of the day and just ensure our products are as functional and as simple as possible. *That which has the greatest use, possesses the greatest beauty.*"

And finally something we could all do well to reflect on, or even sit on: The rocking chair test...

"Every product we make has passed the *rocking chair test*. This is something we use to guide us along the path we are taking. So when we are old and grey and sitting in our rocking chairs, we can look back on the company we created with a smile. That's why we go to the trouble of using the best quality materials to make sure our clothing lasts longer. The longer our products last the less impact they will have on the environment, and the bigger our smile will be."

There's no doubt that most of us will need to take small steps rather than undergo radical change, but I think that if we work collectively we can achieve so much more than on our own:

- By building sustainability into our day-to-day practices and procurement alongside questions about margins and deadlines.

- By asking suppliers to supply information regarding their sourcing and environmental policies. We may be small but many of us use the same suppliers, so collectively we can apply the pressure to improve procurement and product quality.
- By including questions regarding sustainability as part of tenders for shopfitters and other contractors.
- By recording performance and setting targets for sales of recycled, local, Fairtrade and hand-made products in our ranges and working towards increasing these percentages.
- By making choices between like products based on sustainable criteria.
- By sharing information on good suppliers and designers.
- By supplying appropriate information to our customers so that they can make informed choices based on environmental and sustainable criteria.
- By working towards our own sustainability policies and making them available to our customers.
- By championing great design, function and

quality in our products.
·   By keeping sustainability on the *heritage enterprise* agenda.

Ultimately we need to support each other, not only with suppliers, but also to influence our parent institutions, who sometimes see heritage retailing as merely a quick way to achieve some cashflow and not as a meaningful part of the organisation in terms of our values and contribution. All the great heritage and museum retailers have in some way transcended their gift shop status and become an intrinsic part of the brand value of their organisation. I believe more of us can achieve that, but to do so effectively in the future we will have to have sustainability at our heart. I look forward to the challenge ahead and hope we will all be part of a more sustainable and creative future.

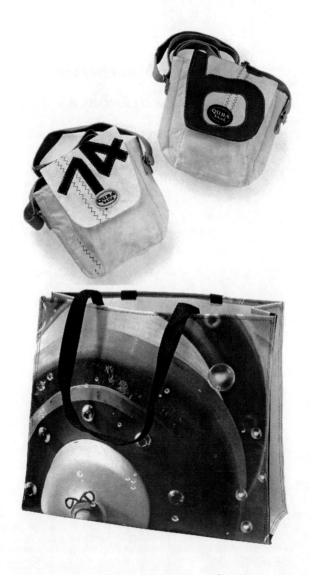

6

Fairtrade in Manchester

MICHAEL WHITWORTH

Head of Commercial Operations

Manchester Museum

For many retail outlets, Fairtrade is perceived as an expensive and risky commitment, and until recent years this was the opinion at Manchester Museum. However, after a major refit, the retail operation of the Museum was making good profits and had established itself as a specialist retailer of unusual gifts from around the globe and was entering an expansion phase with a second shop. This seemed like an ideal opportunity to consider the possibilities provided by becoming a Fairtrade Friendly outlet.

As with any project, the first step was to establish a dedicated team to investigate the viability and criteria for achieving this status. The support of museum staff, Manchester City Council, the Fairtrade Foundation and many of our suppliers was vital in reaching our target of becoming a Fairtrade Friendly outlet.

The project aimed to bring the retail operations of the Museum in line with the ethical stance of the other divisions of the organisation. The Director of the Museum at that time was also Chair of the Museums Association Ethics Committee and was therefore keen for Manchester Museum to set an example. It was also considered to be an important step in the development of the University of Manchester's Fairtrade policy as the Museum is a division of this institution. On a more commercial level it would provide a useful marketing tool in today's ethically aware society. This was especially relevant as a University Museum where it was important to appeal to the staff and students as well as bringing in new customers interested in unusual gifts.

Initially the goal of the project was to have all the stock in the shop supplied by Fairtrade suppliers. However, it soon became clear that this was not viable due to the adverse effects on profitability. The Museum is based in an underprivileged area of the City and the necessary increase in prices would have prohibited many visitors from buying goods from the shop. It was therefore important to strike a balance between helping developing nations and being fair to people from the local area.

The criteria for recognition as a Fairtrade Friendly retail outlet as laid down by Manchester City Council did not require such drastic action. Their desire to maintain their Fairtrade City Status requires that Fairtrade products are readily available in and around the area.

To become Fairtrade Friendly you can[1]:
- stock two or more Fairtrade products[2];
- advertise that you stock Fairtrade[2];
- host an awareness-raising event in your store;
- exclusively use Fairtrade tea and coffee for

meetings;
- have Fairtrade alternatives in vending machines;
- host a tasting session.

It was important for the Museum to achieve more than the bare minimum requirements and so it was decided to stock a mixture of Fairtrade and Ethical trade stock. Therefore the museum shop aimed to have 25% of its products supplied by Fair Traders. It was important for the shop to achieve Fairtrade Friendly status with Manchester City Council as well as providing Fairtrade Certified products as defined by the Fairtrade Foundation.

As Fairtrade is also about development, the generic standards distinguish between minimum requirements which producers must meet to be certified Fairtrade. Process requirements also encourage producer organisations to continuously improve working conditions and product quality, to increase the environmental stability of their activities and to invest in the development of their organisations and the welfare of their producers/workers.

Trading standards stipulate that traders must[3]:
- pay a price to producers that covers the costs of sustainable production and living;

- pay a premium that producers can invest in development;
- make partial advance payments when requested by producers;
- sign contracts that allow for long-term planning and sustainable production practices.

After extensive research, it was decided that all adult giftware sold in the shop would come from Fairtrade sources as this customer sector was willing and able to pay the inevitable slight increase in prices. However, if the children's gifts were provided by Fairtrade suppliers this would have had a major negative effect on profitability, and the number of stock lines would be reduced as there are very few suppliers able to provide children's giftware from Fairtrade sources. Therefore, all children's giftware would be supplied by Ethical Traders. The Museum has a duty to provide a service to existing customers, and therefore children must be able to buy souvenirs on their school trips or visits with their parents. This would not be possible if the less expensive stock lines were discontinued because they could not be supplied by Fairtrade suppliers.

What is the difference between *Fair Trade* and *Ethical Trade*?

Both Ethical Trade and Fair Trade aim to bring real

benefits to the lives of workers in developing countries. Both seek to improve incomes and working conditions. But they differ in the groups of producers and workers they target, and in the methods used to achieve their objectives, as well as in the underlying objectives of the organisations involved in them.

Fair Trade targets disadvantaged communities and organisations working with them, to enable them to be involved in international trade. Fair Trade involves working in partnership with producers to help them build their skills and their capacity to trade more effectively with organisations in developed countries.

The term *Ethical Trade* is now most commonly used to refer to the work of the Ethical Trading Initiative (ETI). This is a partnership of high street companies, NGOs and trade unions, with support from the government. The ETI's aim is to ensure that internationally recognised labour standards, in particular fundamental human rights in the workplace, are observed at all stages in the production of high street goods sold in the UK. The ETI's work is based on standards laid down in Conventions agreed under the International Labour Organisation, which have the force of international law. For more information about the ETI, visit www.ethicaltrade.org.

Oxfam summarises the differences as follows: *We*

hope that one day all goods available in the UK will have been traded according to the standards of the ETI. But Fair Trade is about more than just standards and codes of conduct; it is about working in partnership with disadvantaged groups, helping them to overcome the serious barriers they face in finding a market for the goods they grow or make. Oxfam stocks a range of both fairly and ethically traded products in its shops.[4]

The major task on the road to achieving these goals was to source appropriate products. Initially the recommended suppliers lists made available by the Fair Trade Officer at Manchester City Council and the Fairtrade Foundation were invaluable. Attendance at national giftware fairs and Fairtrade fairs run by the Fairtrade Foundation also provided good leads.

The internet proved to be one of the best tools for finding information and trading partners, since many smaller suppliers are unable to attend major fairs. Organisations such as Oxfam, Shared Earth and the Co-op also provide links to their suppliers' websites as there is a duty for Fairtrade Friendly outlets to promote their suppliers.

Surprisingly, around 25% of the Museum's established suppliers were able to provide Fairtrade products which made the task much easier. It is worthwhile checking with existing suppliers as they do not always

publicise these goods as well as they might. A further
5% of suppliers were willing to change manufacturers
to meet Ethical Trade standards. Although only 30%
of established suppliers were retained, they provided
around half of the stock lines. Had the percentage of
stock lines been lower then it would have been much
more difficult to attain the goal of 25% of stock being
supplied by Fairtrade suppliers.

The achievement of Fairtrade Friendly status has
resulted in a change from the conventional methods
of buying to one which is much more investigative and
time-consuming. Each product must be quality assured
with a paper trail including information such as:

- where is the product from?
- how was it produced?
- who benefits from its production?
- what percentage of the profit goes back to the
  original producer?

Manchester Museum achieved official recognition as
a Fairtrade Friendly retail outlet by Manchester City
Council in August 2006 following an extensive marketing campaign. This included producing posters
promoting Fairtrade products for display both in the
shop and in cases around the Museum., press releases
for the local press and the University in-house maga-

zine, stickers marking Fairtrade products and information panels within the shop detailing the producers
and giving an explanation of Fairtrade. The Museum
chose to launch the new range of products during a
weekend of Fairtrade events held as part of the Fairtrade Fortnight hosted by the Fairtrade Foundation
and Manchester City Council.

Although there is some increase in the amount of
time spent on buying activities, this is offset by the
positive image that having Fairtrade Friendly status
provides, and despite initial concerns the reduction in
profit margins has been offset by increased turnover.

1. *How to be a Fairtrade Friendly Shop/Retail Outlet. Manchester City
Council, 2004.*

2. *Essential criteria for Fairtrade Friendly accreditation*

3. *From the Fairtrade Foundation website: www.fairtrade.org.uk*

4. *From the Oxfam website: www.oxfam.org.uk/shop*

MORE IMAGES: WWW.MUSEUMSETC.COM/?PAGE _ ID=1378

7

Future Retailing

MICHAEL WALTON

Head of Trading

London Transport Museum

What is the world of museum retailing going to look like in ten years time? Of course I have no certain view, but the study of trends and a vigorous interest in the new and fashionable is a worthy brew, and raking over the resulting tea leaves is a pastime that always intrigues me.

Public sector finances can never be relied on to deliver to museums and galleries a never-ending source of funding necessary for the sector to thrive. The public purse is scraped bare by the ever-increasing demands of an ageing population, ever more expensive demands on Health and Education services, as well as the myriad of other agencies eager to prove their collective worth to an ever more sceptical Treasury, or of course, Town Hall.

Former UK Prime Minister, Harold MacMillan, famously said when asked what was his greatest problem in power: "Events dear boy, events". It is events that determine so much of the possible landscape for future funding, and another event of the magnitude of September 11 2001, would have dire consequences on the sector. What too of climate change or a major ecological disaster? The current, and sudden, emergence in Autumn 2008 of the global credit crisis, and its ramifications set to rumble interminably on, is a perfect example of such an event. Where do museums and galleries sit on the priority list? I hope what this illustrates is that national and global events have a relatively speedy effect on the sector's commercial business.

Retail planning for next ten years will have to include many different options for a still fast-changing world, and some of the planning may seem absurd, but I believe it will be vital to have a plan A, B and C depending on the twists and turns of technology, national and world events.

Our retailing world in ten years may look like this: will only the fittest, biggest, cleverest or most esoteric institutions viably survive? If in the "good times" Bury can see fit to sell a Lowry painting, one of its prized possessions, to fund a shortfall in its Social Services budget, what might "bad times" produce? Perhaps many museums and galleries will begin a long march towards forms of Trust status, already achieved by some, but does the rocky road beckon others? Independent Trusts are usually characterised by the increasing influence of stakeholders, and this trend is set to accelerate, as new funding is sought and opportunities identified. As stakeholder influence increases, and funding becomes more problematic, the instincts for survival become more visible: the tightly focused exhibition programme, the high profile lecture series and the important but co-published book.

Retail's part in this world will rest on a true understanding of its role. My erstwhile boss, whenever the subject arose would insist< "Retail is marketing, marketing and marketing. And bad retail is bad marketing". This harshness will shine with increased intensity in ten years' time. Indeed, no directly-run retailing may be a sensible option for some museums. If it is bad marketing, or fails to contribute real return, just stop doing it. Close the operation down, franchise or rent out the space. The same has happened to catering in many museums. Indeed, the future may see other functions outsourced: marketing, security, design, press and public relations. The best defence against an increasing logical - and for some attractive - series of options is to take the widest view of strategic retail planning.

We are all aware of the branding and purpose of key institutions, many of whose identities are burned into the conscious or subconscious of their actual and intended audience. The British Museum, Tate, Imperial War Museum and many others have done fantastic work to build identifiable and reliable brands. And in so doing, I suggest, their core purpose is as clear to them as is the output to their audiences. All image makers know that to maintain core values and certainties and to carefully keep moving the brand forward, are vital to the public's perception of health and fitness for purpose. Successful retail needs successful branding to thrive and, in a decade, retailing should be a partner in that driving seat.

For reasons suggested earlier, efficient cost control and real return will mean a more sustainable retailing operation is essential. Old demarcations of staffing across museums and galleries should be examined in much more depth, ancient structures demolished and replaced by fewer people working more efficiently across more disciplines - and I very much suspect, rather more happily. Small teams of specialists should survive, but working to a far sharper remit. Organisational health checks will, I think, become absolutely essential for whole businesses to thrive in the round. I do not think that future of out-sourcing or possible closure is an idle threat that will, like a morning mist, just evaporate.

Oddly, however, an issue of historically lesser importance to many an institutions' capital funding programmes has been the retail environment. I suggest that the capital costs and quality of planning of such spaces should assume the same importance as a major new gallery. The quality of such spaces should be under constant and critical review. Retail is Marketing.

Museum and gallery retailing has two big new

issues to deal with. In a decade both may assume an importance that we are only beginning to grasp.

As even successful institutions struggle for space and widening audience bases, ever-growing outreach programmes will focus more and more on the young and the old (at schools, colleges, hospitals, clubs and day centres), as well as major outdoor public events. How, if at all, should retailing respond? A mobile shop to follow the outreach programme or a tent at the City Festival? Perhaps yes to one or other or both. I am mindful of the potential dilemmas of the identification of real cost control and the burgeoning expenses and probably modest return of off-site trading in these and other forms. Perhaps this could be achieved with far more effective internal and/or external business partners?

Then, of course, there is the Internet. It is said that those who fail to learn the lessons of history are doomed to repeat them, and with this in mind, I remember in 1984 being lectured with some certainty by a former senior colleague. He objected to the purchase of additional bookshelves with the reasoning that in future books would be replaced by videos. He further foresaw a time in the then near future when books would be kept in, but not sold by, museums. As we all know, the publishing business is alive and videos are, well, museum pieces. As is clear, videos augmented the book business, and indeed can safely be said, created a new and different market, and this market has continued to grow and morph into the DVD business. Where is the next mainstream application of a so-far unknown technology? None of this has taken place at the expense of traditional publishing, which, benefiting from new technology, has prospered and developed. The analogy is true of the Internet.

The inexorable rise of Internet retailing has attracted siren calls of commentators preparing us for the death of traditional retailing, and a brave bold new world of home shopping. Alluding to the video analogy, the Internet is indeed a brave new world, but will largely exist and develop in parallel with the traditional role of the High Street. New breeds of customers are emerging. The super specialist able to search for everything in their chosen interest range; the time poor and asset rich; the Internet junkie; those too far away to ever visit. I am sure there are more identifiable groups that exist and yet more that will emerge. These are different and new markets, and strategies to address these markets will occupy much time and effort. Certainly from our experience - hard won in some ways - the customer expectation of next day or two day delivery has been a tough challenge to consistently deliver. With what resources do you plan for these markets or is it best to pay limited attention and concentrate on the known retailing world?

I believe in ten years, successful museum and gallery retailing will have developed two parallel trading businesses, one cyber and one actual. Both will be interlinked with a number of key common denominators. What these will be will not be easy to predict. Different institutions will have different objectives, but the key determinants will include those products which can project brand and brand values most strongly and with clarity of purpose to the widest market. For the Tate group, most products, both own label and generic, may be suitable for sale in both their shops and on the Internet, but perhaps for others a more specialist offer might be appropriate. It is, and will be, best to consider the Internet and traditional retailing as two windows, perhaps with different "displays", to the same operation.

With the Internet comes the allied ideas of print-on-demand and a variety of new methods of selling and fulfilment. Print-on-demand, usually though a third party provider, is becoming increasingly interesting. Widening out the collection to a greater audience has commercial benefits, but museums and galleries will need to work more closely together to gain economies of scale for printing and fulfilment. At present, revenues accruing to institutions from this work are modest.

London Transport Museum has recently worked with an Internet provider to develop a new secure order system which allows the customer to pre-order a selection of special items, which are then manufactured to order, and despatched after bank accounts have been automatically debited. All customer account information is held in a secure suspension account by the partner bank, and fulfilment is to the Museum's timetable. I think this also provides a model for future despatch systems. Using this tool, we can decide what item is developed by us or a third party, and who arranges its delivery, to where, and despatched by whom. We think we have discovered an immensely flexible way to develop both our actual and cyber businesses. Whether this becomes a generic museums and galleries business model, I remain uncertain, but its apparent capability suggests a huge additional business investment to exploit the anticipated flexibility.

Out of cyberspace and into the now exquisite ambience of the real shop, who is the customer we are likely to see, and what will they buy? The typical shopper is becoming wealthier, less bothered by buying stuff, as they probably have too much of it. They are increasingly interested in big ticket items; perhaps a holiday home; a third or much better car, eating out once, twice, more a week, a new bathroom or a landscape gardener. Consumer focus will be increasingly on goods that mean something to the purchaser or purchased for, and I foresee a huge growth in the authority of the sector for the *bought for children* market. The provenance of food and drink will also provide tremendous opportunity for some in ten years time. From farm to museum shop. As long as this business is justified in the remit, what is the issue?

Product development is an expensive and time consuming pastime. It is easy to just apply a brand on a generic plain product, and with it you may get by. But all product emanating from the disparate collection of renowned institutions must convey conviction in the brand as well as the product itself. In ten years, successful retailing will demand excellent product development, not only from the established collections, but I rather hope from a new breadth of cultural commissioning that is appropriate to the institution. To meet the challenges of an ever more homogenised, process-driven world, it would be good to believe that our sector is busy commissioning future art, objects, toys or whatever which become used in a highly responsible and commercially adept manner. If retailing was all about marketing, then in future it will be also about innovation.

Innovation has a price, sometimes a hefty one. Product development will become a key - and cross-functional - requirement in ten years, where postholders will influence marketing, retail, exhibition planning and design, stakeholder relations, and of course, as we must I think, prepare for in ten years time, partners.

As large companies try to negate the many environmental and financial issues that will, I believe, press heavier and heavier on Boardroom agendas, one of the ways in which our sector can make a real difference to the corporate world is to find appropriate partners. Appropriately branded cross-selling, and the careful management of brand values will possibly provide an entirely new and purposeful future.

The future must also be fun. It must carry authority and be of the highest quality. It needs constant investment and nourishment if it is not to die. It must be about marketing, brand values, innovation, stakeholders, partners, Internet, outreach and efficiency. It needs to cost less and earn more. It needs to be relevant.

I look forward to the future, and particularly to the article or lecture that repudiates this view, and points to an altogether different world. It seems right to finish this article by saying: *Hello!*

8

Successful Temporary Retail

Head of Retail Strategy & Operations

Natural History Museum, London

Shopping isn't always the first thing on a visitor's mind after walking round an exhibition. But with good forward planning, a handful of new ideas and a lot of past experience, my team at the Natural History Museum has developed a few golden rules for making a retail offer work.

Temporary exhibitions come in many shapes and sizes: hired touring exhibitions, those created in-house, ticketed, free, adult–focused, fun for kids. The list is endless. While each needs to be as good an experience as possible for the visitor, reflecting the museum and its work and being appropriate to the audience, the retail offer also needs to be tailored. Having said that, we come to golden rule number one. Never put a shop after an exhibition, just because you think you should. Only if it can be proved the shop will be profitable should it be developed. And it is never too early to start that.

The number of visitors you can expect to an exhibition depends on the total number of visitors and how popular the content will be. For example, at the Natural History Museum, we'd expect more people to a Dinosaurs exhibition in the summer than an exhibition on Hair. Ideally, any retail operation linked to a temporary exhibition should be located at the exit from the exhibit, although guidebook and disposable camera sales opportunities should not be missed at the entrance. Once visitor numbers to the exhibition are forecast, you can work out the number of customers to expect in the shop. The Natural History Museum works to an average 20% conversion rate for exhibition shops. The starting point for establishing projected levels of turnover within the shop is the Average Transaction Value (ATV) of each purchase made. This is calculated by looking at the prices of products ranged within the shop and the likely combinations to be purchased by any one customer. Then the forecasted number of transactions multiplied by ATV will give the total forecasted turnover (Gross) for the shop.

Once proved that it will be profitable, the range planning can begin. The range of merchandise in the shop will be determined by the target audience of the exhibition and the content. If the target audience is predominantly adult, then the ATV is likely to be higher than if it is an exhibition targeted at children – books and jewellery are more expensive than novelty erasers and jigsaws. Having said that, the total number of transactions is likely to be fewer, due to the lack of *pester power*. When planning any merchandise for a temporary exhibition, the most important factor is whether the product can be incorporated in your normal merchandise range after the exhibition ends.

This is key, as most temporary exhibitions result in surplus stock given their limited opening time. If this is not taken into consideration, it can and will use up a lot of valuable markdown budget to clear the stock, which will have a negative impact on the overall margin. Alternatively, initial prices can be set at a high enough level that the margin allows for high future markdowns.

Just as our audience is diverse, so the products are diverse, so the products you choose should appeal to a diverse range of tastes. We have had great success in mixing high end, *wow factor* pieces with pocket money purchases. As part of the range, it is recommended to include a *wow factor* at a high price point. This can be on a sale or return basis with a supplier, but raises the profile and credibility of the range. A wow piece, may also gain valuable PR for the exhibition. For our *Dino Jaws* exhibition we did exactly that and ranged a £250 replica T.rex skull as a wow piece within the exhibition shop and experienced excellent sales. The lesson we have learned from this is that visitors are prepared to purchase high price point pieces, if they are relevant to the exhibition and that they are clearly displayed as a high value item.

Whatever the content of a temporary exhibition, it is vital that the whole exhibition and all retail products relating to that exhibition, share the same brand values. At the Natural History Museum, we always try to ensure that the exhibitions and all stock in exhibition shops, are clear, compelling, fun and offer learning opportunities where possible; in line with the Museum's core brand values.

Shifting your gaze to manufacture abroad is not so much a rule, but something good to consider. If timescales permit and predicted volumes justify the decision, it is far more cost-effective to get large volumes of merchandise manufactured abroad. This often requires the exhibition logo and marketing design to be available very early - this can be a challenge but is not impossible. Alternatively, don't forget to ask around the industry: someone, somewhere will be able to recommend suitable manufacturers who can manufacture high quality product at reasonable prices. Branding is good to a degree, but we've learnt from our mistakes and avoid using the exhibition dates on any products – a dead giveaway after the exhibition has closed. We have developed the facility to sell exhibition related product to touring venues, who are then saved the time and effort in product development.

Looking the part speaks volumes to the customer. Shabby shops say shabby products, so try and factor in good shopfit design to your retail planning. If you are lucky enough to have a budget to design and purchase a new shopfit or fixtures, think ahead to future exhibition needs, in order to ensure flexibility, to get the most out of it. The majority of venues will expect a minimum of three years' life out of fixtures, so durability is also key. You can buy additional perspex trays and troughs on an exhibition by exhibition basis, depending on the needs of the shop. Access around the shop is an essential consideration in conjunction with strong directional lighting, that can be re-directed in future shops.

Our most recent success to date has been the Print on Demand service used with our *Shell Wildlife Photographer of the Year* exhibition. This enables visitors to the exhibition to select an image they like from the exhibition and have it framed in a size and material of their choice, as a lasting memory of the exhibition. This concept can then be marketed to other venues if the exhibition goes on tour, operated in partnership with an external publishing company.

Staff costs are a major cost in temporary exhibition shops, but these can be minimised by planning rotas in line with known visitor patterns and dwell times. Working closely with the front-of-house team is also key, enabling multi-selling wherever possible and minimising the number of people you need. Teamwork between the exhibition designers, engineers, project managers and the retail team is vital. The whole team is working to key deadlines with a common goal, but it is important to ensure that plenty of time is left before opening to merchandise the shop. The role that retail plays in generating incremental income from a temporary exhibition cannot be underestimated and the project management team must ensure it is included as a core part of the overall project plan. With the large number of temporary exhibitions that the Natural History Museum has held over the years, this is now a finally-tuned operation. All this planning, costing and organising goes on without the visitor even knowing. But if they are in the shop, your work is done.

ALIVE TO CHANGE

MORE IMAGES: WWW.MUSEUMSETC.COM/?PAGE _ ID=1378

9

Increasing Visitor Spend

NUALA MCGOURTY

Retail Director

Royal Collection Enterprises

Against a background of disparate inflation measures, where consumers' perception of value appear to be shifting, we can be sure that certain costs will grow relentlessly, despite our best efforts to control them. Salaries, employment costs, utilities, overheads all tend to come into this category and retail profitability has to grow at least as fast as these to maintain, let alone improve, the contribution it delivers. For this reason increasing the spend per visitor and improving transaction values are a critical objective.

For many institutions, the advent of free admissions has proved extremely challenging. It was meant to herald huge increases in visitor numbers, wider access for all, and a consequential switch in spend from admissions income to retail. For a variety of reasons, this did not happen to anything like the extent anticipated and experience seems to indicate that the consumer who visits an institution simply because of a free admission policy, does not spend as much as a visitor who has paid for access. The result, in many cases, is a very diverse visitor mix and reducing spend per head, which together makes a difficult mix for retailers. Do they reduce the average price of the offer to accommodate this trend and hope for increased volumes, or seek to meet their budgets by selling more items to fewer customers?

Whilst The Royal Collection does not fall into this category as it does not operate a free admissions policy, it competes in a market that does, and, likewise, diligently measures its spend per visitor. If this does not meet inflation year on year it can often spell trouble as there are underlying costs associated with any selling transaction that will most probably be growing regardless. And whilst there can always be one-off reasons for a high turnover figure but a low spend per head (for example disproportionately high visitor numbers), a downward trend of average spend can indicate an even greater problem. Are we creating the deflation ourselves by offering the visitor cheaper and cheaper goods?

Improving the average spend per visitor, increasing transaction values and improving customer conversion rates are therefore the key to growing an enduring healthy business in this environment.

The first step towards achieving this is to look at the full extent of the visit and not just polarise on the shop. In many instances the customer service starts long before the visit when information is sought over the telephone or internet and tickets are perhaps purchased in advance. A perfect opportunity exists at this early stage to offer a guidebook in preparation for the trip.

The next stage to interact with your customer is on arrival. Queuing for admission or security search has become almost the norm now for access to any major venue and this offers a further opportunity to offer guidebooks, and, in the case of large outdoor sites, items that people frequently purchase on an *ad hoc* basis - water on a hot day, an umbrella on a wet one.

As the visitor progresses through the site to the shop, it is vital that we as retailers understand what they have experienced. If there is an audio guide, which items are highlighted? What rooms or exhibits never fail to capture their imagination? What are our own special iconic images? We must understand these if we wish to engage with the visitor and convert them into a customer.

Product is of course king in any retail outlet and when developing product we should always strive to follow certain rules. First, is it relevant to the site and is the relevance obvious. Second, are we able to present it effectively in our retail environment for visitors to see it, want it, handle it and buy it? Investment in shop design and fixturing is frequently one of the casualties of financial constraints but increasingly this is a false economy. Customers are now much more sophisticated and they simply will not shop a tired environment, no matter how quaintly old-fashioned we might believe it to be - they will assume that the product is equally as outdated.

At this stage we are trying to improve our customer conversion rates by getting more visitors inside the store in order to sell to them. A three second glance appraising the overall offer informs their decision to cross the threshold, so yes, first impressions do count. Wall graphics, photography, strong clean displays, good lighting, effective signage, and of course staff are all key in highlighting the offer, communicating a brand identity, and generally creating an impression.

Assuming that we are successful in luring a visitor in, we then look at ways to optimise the transaction value. Even the most attractive shop with marvellous product well-displayed and competitively priced can be faced with customers being unable to decide, such is the plethora of choice. Following the 80/20 rule, we must define the best sellers for the customer and promote them accordingly. Most heritage sites operate in an environment where the majority of visitors are tourists or non-regulars which gives them the opportunity to work with proven best sellers which may last two or three years, and avoid product development for its own sake which is always high risk for the first season.

Range development must also be managed with care. A variety of differing items requires the customer to select in an either/or way. Ranges of products in the same family, however, invite customers to buy more than one item on the basis that something matches with their choice - this is obviously easier to display and promote. Point-of-sale material explaining the provenance of an item enhances the relevance and the uniqueness of the offer whist staff - as in any retail outlet - can make or kill the sale.

Baskets are often overlooked as the simplest way of encouraging multiple purchases. As in a supermarket, once a basket is in one's hand, there is a natural temptation to purchase more and staff should always take note of visitors who have taken a basket as it indicates a tacit willingness to buy.

Till points are another way to bulk up a transaction as a customer has, at this point, committed to purchase. They are a good site for promotions, pick-up items and things that could be viewed as "always useful". Clever fixturing can add significant stock density here, in what is otherwise redundant space.

Assuming that we now have a customer with a guidebook, an umbrella, a souvenir plus something that matches it, a biro and packet of mints purchased from the till, we have managed to hit a transaction value of over £20. The lucky venue that has catering will then route the visitor towards the café, where they can review their visit, admire their purchases and enjoy a welcome sit down with, of course, the associated spend. If that's not possible, an ice cream and a bench has proved extremely successful for us, and added a further £2.00 to the day's transaction.

With our market research showing a very impressive value-for-money rating, visitors clearly didn't mind spending their money – they just needed a little help doing so!

10

Five Steps to Retail Success

KATE BULL

Director, CTWB Ltd

"Retail should be easy... It's not exactly rocket science," is a favourite quote of the Managing Director of a well-known retail chain. If that's true, how come so many places get it wrong?

An exciting retail shop is a great opportunity to reinforce the visitors' experience and enable them to take home a piece of your magic - Disney does this so well. As some readers might find the mention of Disney a bit hard to stomach, another example would be the Museum of Modern Art in New York. Its products have become the ubiquitous sign of good taste.

The success of these organisations is based on a set of simple guidelines that every retailer, no matter how small or new, can follow.

The first step is to really understand what you want to achieve - not just what is in your business plan in terms of sales, budgets and profit. But also the wider, less tangible attributes. Like what makes it unique and interesting; what experience you want your visitors to have; what keeps people coming back?

Some of this may be already in the form of a mission statement or possibly a set of brand values or brand behaviours. Great retailers are able to translate these fine words into actions through their products, packaging and environments, and to embody very clearly what they stand for.

Let me give you an example. When I was working for the Southbank Centre (SBC) in London to help it establish its retail strategy, I encouraged the team to focus on what makes the SBC unique. Three key points of difference were identified: the broad range of cultural and artistic experiences to be found on the site; that fact that it was the location for the Festival of Britain in 1951 which was once described as being "....educational, whimsical and slightly kitsch"; and - because the SBC is publicly funded - the commitment to promote London and Britain to the public.

These differences were then used to inform the personality of the shop - its design, products, customer service and even its recruitment of employees – and they continue to be used in this way today. The shop design, for example, incorporates the famous "net and ball" design of the Festival of Britain into the vinyl wall coverings and the 1960s aesthetics of "truth in materials" of the Hayward Gallery in the lighting and finishes around the till point.

Every shop space is different, which is great, but precludes a blueprint for design and layout. When planning the space, you need to ensure accessibility for all customers (meeting DDA requirements). Secondly, take time to consider the customer's journey around the store. At the SBC, the space is divided into distinct areas – the music area, the art area, the children's corner. To maintain the interest of regular customers (many pass by on their way to work), the SBC has a wall of products which are constantly changed to keep it in line with events at the SBC or seasonal events. This also serves to reinforce its links with the Centre, which is especially important given the shop's unique, standalone position.

When placing the tills, make sure they are easy to find and have adequate wrapping space. The fitments and finishes are the canvas for your displays and products.

The surfaces need to be durable and have straightforward cleaning instructions. The feel can be as cluttered or as simple as you like. Clutter works well in an antique shop, for example, where people like to ferret around and find the hidden "treasure". In contrast, the crisp, clean formality of shops like Gap works well for their customers who want to find things easily. Whatever the look and feel, the signage and point of sale décor should be readable and consistent in font sizing, expression of detail and price representation.

Having decided how you want to express yourself through the shop, now comes a tricky part. You have to turn your visitors into customers. Put yourself in their shoes, but don't judge their tastes or the size of their wallets - be open minded.

I appreciate it's hard to remove one's own opinions when buying stock, but this is a common mistake. All too often people stock up on items they would like to buy, rather than what customers actually want to buy. I recently visited a stately home and safari park, and was surprised to find a display of baby clothes alongside the fluffy animals in the park shop. This out-of-place merchandise was bought solely because the manager had recently become a mother. As mentioned earlier, it is essential to keep at the heart of your product choices the core values of the heritage centre.

I visit many museums and their shops and it is often very obvious to see the long reach of curator's arm. This is most frequently expressed by the imbalance of the product ranges - typically with either too many items or too many high-priced products. To create a cohesive range, you need to know how many different styles or types of items you can display, how much volume of stock you need to fill the display and what your price range is. Thereby ensuring there is something accessible for everybody who visits the shop. For example, a children's range could have up to 85% of its wares selling at under £5 aimed at pocket money purchases. You should also look to keep the number price breaks sensible and consistent to aid the customer.

Museums and heritage centres, by definition, have deep connections with the past, but we are all influenced by the present. Outside forces - such as politics, the economy and the weather locally, nationally or worldwide - have a direct effect on our business and customers. The current influx of cheap goods makes it impossible to walk into any gift shop and not find a Chinese-made product.

Contrast this with the growing groundswell of consumer desire for green, locally-sourced and ethically-produced items. The *Duchy* range of organic products and its worldwide success demonstrates how big the market can be. Returning to the SBC, the innovative inclusion of original 1950s pieces, British-designed recycled products, and the commissioning of new designers, is proving to be an alternative way to satisfy to this need.

And, finally, with regard to product offerings, don't forget the events that happen every year: Christmas, Valentine's Day, Mothering Sunday, Easter, Father's Day and the school holidays. You can piggy-back off these to boost sales and create a flow of timely new products.

To facilitate the buying process, keep accurate records of each line and how it is selling. However, information will only be of use if you keep it up-to-date, review regularly and feed your findings back into the strategy. In just the same way as we eat with our eyes, customers buy with their eyes!

Investing in really good visual merchandise support is never wasted. The skills for effectively showing products are very different from those of showcasing art works. Beware of the glass case method of display finding its way into the shop from the gallery, showing precious products that transfix the viewers with such awe that they struggle to get to the till. Or, worse still, inhibiting them from buying the items because they can't touch or feel them. If you want inspiration visit *Fortnum & Mason* in London's Piccadilly to see the best. Here the retailer's passion for the products it sells is almost tangible – every tin faces the right way, every label is in the right place – the attention to detail is outstanding.

Your trump card is your people. The best shops will employ the best sales assistants and managers. These people are recruited on their ability to positively interact with customers, their personal motivation and their eye for detail. This enthusiastic group of people deserve good, attentive management. Retail is a fast-paced environment and the ability to make timely decisions is vital.

The final step to retail success is to have a good

knowledge of your competitors and to be aware of the best and the worst. Visiting local shops with your staff is an easy way to see what can be done. Some ordinary shops are beautifully presented, and give instant demonstrations how displays of quite mundane items can be shown.

It's true, retail is not rocket science. It is a combination of detailed planning, excellent team work, a gentle touch of creativity and the ability to react quickly to ensure success.

11

Retail Evolution

IAIN BETTERTON

Commercial Manager

Dulwich Picture Gallery

Dulwich Picture Gallery is one of London's most amazing treasures. Sir John Soane's building of 1811, the first purpose-built public art gallery in England and the blueprint for all subsequent efforts, provides plenty of wow factor alone. Its marriage to the Rick Mather extension, completed in 2000, juxtaposes outstanding architectural achievements two hundred years apart. Inside, time appears to stop. The original collection, whose founders still keep an eye on proceedings from their final resting places within the Mausoleum, commands the visitor back in time, striking wonder and awe, as only the likes of Rembrandt and the "divine" Guido Reni can. Dulwich Picture Gallery is small but perfectly formed and delivers a knock-out punch every time. For several years the Gallery has been my place of work but there has been no erosion in my appreciation of its arts: it never loses the capacity to hush a busy mind and elicit wonder, even when pushing a trolley-full of catalogues to the shelves.

Congratulations, then, are due to the architects Sir John and Rick, founders Noel Desenfans, Francis Bourgeois and Margaret Desenfans, Directors past and present all for making and keeping Dulwich Picture Gallery alive where other less loved, less well-managed institutions would have crumbled into a state of disrepair. The building and the pictures have not always had it so good, and time has tested them, especially when a German bomb arrived in 1944; but restoration projects, always a vital part of the upkeep of any national treasure, have never been so prolific at the Gallery as they are today.

Visitors simply gorge themselves on the unique look and feel of the place, but they are never satiated until that particular piece of the Gallery which twinkled brightest in their eyes makes it home with them in some form or other. This is why shops in the cultural environment have a head-start on the high street – their visitors have been uniquely stimulated and their appetites are the larger for it. Their specific, peculiar type of need can only be fixed here and now, not tomorrow in Bluewater or Tesco's. If Rembrandt's *Girl at a Window* gives you a knowing glance and you want to reciprocate, then why not continue that promising relationship by taking her home with you and sticking her on your fridge? It's all about preservation, bottling the emotion, capturing a meaningful experience. And, it's Mum's birthday next week and wouldn't Uncle Fred simply die for one of those? If *Girl at a Window* is the main course, why not a card pack for starters, a mounted print for pudding and that neat little gift-book at the counter for coffee? Stimulate, then satiate. Or for the more cynically-minded: poison, then offer the antidote.

In retail, as in life itself, survival of the fittest is no glib cliché – put the right product, fairly priced, in front of your customers, and they will, given a conducive environment, consume. Fail to understand why they are in your retail space in the first place, neglect to evolve with their changing expectations, and extinction looms. We evolve through making mistakes, finding out what works, and constant monitoring of performance. And we take calculated risks, all the time understanding that our business peaks and troughs as exhibitions come and go, making knee-jerk evaluations brittle assumptions at best.

Dulwich Picture Gallery has evolved to keep its head above water, busy protecting the very things that make it worth preserving – the building and the collection, and a window into that capsule of time to which it belongs. The retail offer matters, now more than ever, in reaching out to new audiences, and underpinning the financial stability of the enterprise. It is obvious when you look at the larger museums and galleries that retail is a central part of the visitor experience, not merely a peripheral one. Increasingly, one shop is not enough. We want the flagship store, the post-exhibition outlet and a bookshop.

Most people regard evolution as inherently linked to size: the bigger, the better, the more advanced.

But compare your local greengrocer to your nearest supermarket – which makes you feel more valued? And remember what happened to those gigantic dinosaurs. Evolving the retail offer is all about being smarter, not necessarily bigger. Of course, if you're smart enough for long enough in the retail world, you do tend to increase in size. The shop at Dulwich Picture Gallery is small – around 450 square feet. Nothing, except a new build, or a mezzanine floor, will alter that fact. This is our unique constraint to the next evolutionary step.

If there are awards aplenty for the pictures and the architecture then I'm afraid a large wooden spoon goes for the retail provision which arrived as a bit of an afterthought. The shop was shoe-horned into the entrance room of the Gallery, once the space reserved for the crown jewels of the collection, becoming a thoroughfare in and out, with ticket sales bullying space away from the retail offer and making for the kind of browsing experience you'd expect to find at Heathrow Airport's Terminal 5. As the main entrance and exit to the Gallery, the shop became a real bottleneck, flooded whenever a coach party turned up. It put people off browsing, impinged on display potential and created a poor first impression of the Dulwich experience.

Over the past few years, the retail environment at

Dulwich Picture Gallery has evolved, slowly at first during an evaluation phase, but then more suddenly as opportunities for change arose. From ousting interpretation boards, reclaiming space for product, and condensing displays, to introducing a full range of greetings cards, jewellery for the first time and a custom print service, little by little we responded to our customers' wishes, steadily improving our conversion rates. We looked at product unsparingly, increasing the presence of our most popular and profitable departments and refreshing or consigning stale ranges to history. Progress was steady without being spectacular.

On the eve of *Canaletto in England*, an exhibition from January 2007 which promised record visitor numbers, we chose to take a pro-active evolutionary step. On arrival, visitors were redirected away from the shop towards a secondary entrance at the side of the building. They queued in Rick's wonderful glass cloister, entered the Gallery at the north end, swept through exhibition rooms, back up through the enfilade shimmering with nuggets from the permanent collection and out via the shop. The blood flow had been diverted, and we strengthened accordingly.

As a direct result of this initiative, other changes fell into place like dominos. A second shop till was introduced where entrance tickets had been sold. Suddenly we found our capacity for dealing with customers greatly increased, from an average of 3,400 transactions a month to 4,400. Our previous monthly record of 5,400 transactions was dwarfed by a new total of 9,150. No unsightly queues, and no potential customers putting their chosen items back on the shelves.

The evolution was not just in terms of efficiency either. The shop warmed to the new emphasis and developed point-of-sale units, a poster browser, and a narrowing of the new entrance into the shop from the enfilade rather than the grounds, enclosing the shopping environment and inviting people to stay and explore before leaving. This new skin allowed another process, which had been improving steadily, to flourish – namely the range of merchandise. With new units and extra space, exhibition-related product, responsible for between 40% and 45% of our business, could be given greater breadth and visual potency. In between shows, a brighter mix of design-led items seemed to create our very own set of retail jewels on the new acrylic units which increased the display area without ever crowding the space. Arise the Pantone Mug, you are a Gallery product now. Our DNA has been altering, delivering new aspirations. We are stronger, in look and feel and on the bottom line. Our customers appear satisfied (for now); and we want to keep them drooling.

Results have been impressive for the new sleeker, smarter shop – in the same small room, but with a different pulse. The December following, *Canaletto in England* was a real triumph – more visitors became customers than didn't, a conversion rate exceeding 50.4%. The shop is still thriving, and customers are satisfied, but this is simply one evolutionary step. Whilst we are congratulating ourselves on being able to smash open nuts with a large rock, our neighbours are, admittedly with more resources, busily inventing the wheel. The process does not stop, and must remain fluid to achieve optimum results given the available resources. A licensing programme, a dynamic online offer, a mail order catalogue – the areas for growth are greater than our ability to fill them, currently – but over time, and with smart decisions, and the right retail offer, Dulwich Picture Gallery will continue to take enterprising strides.

B LUXMOORE

MORE IMAGES: WWW.MUSEUMSETC.COM/?PAGE _ ID=1378

12

Retail in a Recession

PETER TULLIN &

SIMON CRONSHAW

Joint Founders,

CultureLabel.com

Today's recession is accelerating nothing short of a revolution in retail. Cloned beyond character, the high street is facing a miserable future as customers migrate online in their millions in search of the convenience, choice and value established by shopping on the web. Survey after survey confirms the trend: as a typical indicator, in June 2009 Experian forecasted UK online retail spend to grow by as much as £12.3bn, to £21.3bn, by the end of 2011. At present nearly nine million adults shop online at least once a week; overall £1 pound in every £14 will be spent online by 2012 according to Experian's predictions.

High street stalwart Marks and Spencer revealed its online sales were up 29% in the 13 weeks to 27 December 2008 despite one of its worst Christmas trading periods, with UK like-for-like sales down 7.1%. The retail landscape is fundamentally shifting. PricewaterhouseCoopers forecast that online shopping will grow from £20 billion today to £50 billion in 2012 (UK). The evidence goes on...

There's no going back, as demonstrated by the remodelling of entire industries, including music and fashion, to cater for new consumer preferences which favour online purchasing. Less than ten years ago, sceptical observers were adamant that clothes could never be bought online: it was all in the physical

ALIVE TO CHANGE

"touch". Yet in the year ending March 2008, fashion retailer asos saw sales reach £81 million, up ten-fold in just four years. For Christmas 2008, asos defied high street gloom with sales soaring 118% year-on-year in the nine weeks to 16 January and sales for the 42 weeks to 16 January up 108%. The site attracted 5.2 million unique visitors in December alone.

Moreover, fashion retailers have inadvertently fostered new consumer behaviours: buy regularly then return without hesitation if necessary. Consumers have evolved to incorporate the quirks of the online sales process. Try telling your typical asos customer to wait until their next lunch hour to trudge into town in search of that elusive weekend outfit. Virtually infinite choice plus instant stock availability awaits online. Would you really ever go back to the high street?

Offline feast
Set these developments against the boom in culture merchandise and artist-designed product, on the back of a significant growth and mainstreaming of cultural consumption in the UK. Such fires are fuelled by a combination of the National Lottery, a general growth in public funding, and shifting consumer trends including the demand for authentic experiences.

The recession has crystallized this, with a number

of commentators characterising the last ten years as a golden age for culture, and the headlines really are staggering. Tate is now the most popular contemporary art gallery in the world. The *Superbrands 2008* survey revealed that the very same organisation is now a more powerful brand in the eyes of consumers than both Vodafone and Manchester United. As if to confirm the mainstreaming of cultural consumption, Futurelab revealed that on one day during the Weather Project by Olafur Eliasson there were more visitors in Tate Modern than Bluewater, Europe's largest shopping centre. No wonder the shop's doing well, we hear you cry! Tate Modern covers 34,000 square metres, while Bluewater extends to 154,000. Things came full circle when the commercial operators of the O2 opened the Bubble to host exhibitions such as *Tutankhamen*, selling over a million tickets to outstrip the British Museum's *First Emperor* as the largest paid-for exhibition.

Over the last few years, retail has increasingly borrowed from the practices of artists and cultural institutions to deliver better experiences, environment and product - as a trip to any branch of Urban Outfitters will confirm. It is far more questionable how much the culture sector has imported from the retail sector in return. This is starting to change with players such as the National Trust expanding their high street presence.

And the nascent growth in licensing is delivering Natural History Museum children's clothing to M&S and V&A secateurs to John Lewis. The Science Museum's annual licensing turnover has now reached £16 million, selling items through high street retailers including Argos and WHSmith. On the global stage, meanwhile, MoMA recently expanded its Design Store platform to Tokyo to great critical and commercial acclaim.

As another culture superbrand, the Metropolitan Museum now has a staggering 32 stores worldwide, and was voted in *Zagat* to be the fifth most popular department store in New York. Innovative collaborations with commercial brands have also helped to improve product ranges. As sponsorship increasingly morphs into cultural branding, more commercial brands look to product creation with merchandise or culture content alongside cultural institutions as a win-win revenue source. Premium products recently emerging in this way include the Reality Bag (Puma and the Serpentine Gallery) and the Ultimate Travel Suit (Ted Baker and London Transport Museum).

It's not just the big boys, however. The growth of niche markets has allowed institutions such as the Jackfield Tile Museum (part of the Ironbridge Gorge Museum Trust) to form partnerships with retailers such as Fired Earth in order to find a marketplace for the stunning product that has been inspired by their Designated Collection of tile designs.

Online famine

Whilst offline culture retail is steadily developing, e-commerce in the culture sector is disappointing. According to CultureLabel.com research, online trading ran between 1-3% of turnover on average for even the largest museums and galleries (although there were some strong performers bucking this trend, such as the Design Museum).

Given the phenomenal growth in online retail, and the adaption of consumer behaviour to incorporate multi-channel buying, this is remarkable. The industry average for online penetration in comparable sectors floats around 20%, and could account for as much as 50% by 2014 [1]. Not many retailers could report double digit growth on the high street over Christmas 2008, and the growth curve (rising since 2002) is not expected to plateau until at least 2016. Significant opportunities are being missed by culture institutions.

Consumer insight is as important in this narrative as the capacity of the culture sector when considering e-commerce. Unlike *ethical shopping* and *alternative gifts*, there is currently no *cultural shopping* category in the minds of many consumers, meaning that culture products are often bypassed by consumers on their purchasing journey online. Oxfam Unwrapped demonstrated spectacular sales growth when it helped shape a compelling new *ethical merchandise* consumer category, using a powerful celebrity-backed campaign with the iconic call to buy shares in a donkey!

Other businesses such as Ethicalsuperstore.com have benefited from the birth of the ethical merchandise category (or Google search phrase more importantly) and aggregated a group of powerful brands to connect more directly with consumers who prefer shopping according to lifestyle choice. This site recorded a 50% year-on-year increase in sales in December to £500,000, and saw sales in the first fortnight of January 2009 up 60 per cent – revealing the power of targeted online campaigns to specific consumer tribes, even in the recession.

Aggregation of cultural institutions is the means by which the sector can make it effortless for the consumer to discover you and browse the widest possible range. With Google as king, aggregation represents a major boost to organic search optimisation, enabling institutions to rise through the ranks of generic search listings preferred by mainstream consumers. Lates, a website that allows people to search across the details of late-night openings of a group of leading organisations in London, is perhaps one of the best examples of aggregation in the sector. The brand is clearly targeted at the 18-35 demographic, an audience that is keen to consume culture on its own terms. It has attracted significant interest from brand partners including FCUK, Apple and Sony PlayStation as a result - not your traditional art sponsors.

Launching in July 2009, CultureLabel.com delivers the benefits of aggregation and sophisticated onsite merchandising to retailers in the arts and culture sector.

Merchandise, artist-designed products, editions, tickets, experiences and memberships will be available from a wide range of leading global and UK culture institutions through a single retail portal for the first time. (Post plug, we should point out here that we are behind this particular venture among others.)

However, despite this shameless self-promotion, we bring it up in order to flag up the enormous task of building a new marketplace and product category. Our vision was to create a platform that was entirely consumer-facing and positioned on the purchasing journey, rather than the typical positioning as adjunct to a visitor web journey; the challenge most institution e-shops face.

Context aside, we would now like to share just a handful of the ideas and sites that have shaped our own development over the last 18 months.

Always connected

The advent of the smartphone is now connecting product to place in ways that were previously not possible (or, as with most things mobile web, too annoying to bother with). On average only 10% of mobile phone users surf the web. This is perhaps not surprising given that the common experience seems to revolve around furiously smashing your phone pad and then, after several attempts, finally managing to crank out a few unfulfilling pages on a tiny screen. However, this reality is changing rapidly with O2 reporting that this figure for mobile surfing is nearer 80% for owners of the iPhone. Could it be that with the unveiling of a new range of smartphones such as Google's G1 specifically built for internet browsing, the age of mobile marketing may finally have dawned?

More importantly, the software is also undergoing something of a revolution. The world of iPhone apps is booming with more than 300 million applications downloaded from the iTunes store in just six months. Someone brighter than us did the maths to work out the staggering statistic that 13 million iPhone users have downloaded as much software as 1.1 billion conventional mobiles (in terms of market share).

Google's Android platform is well-positioned to power the G1 community and this could provide some healthy competition and drive these figures yet higher, turning your phone into an ever-ready mobile shop attached to you at all times. The stuff of dreams for those who admit to buying more as dwell time on the net continues to increase. Add in GPS and Bluetooth and you have the ability to hit customers with targeted, location-sensitive services.

Social shopping

Flickr, MySpace, Facebook, Bebo, LinkedIn and Twitter have all demonstrated the power of social networks to create communities of interest which can fuel anything from music sales to super-specific targeted advertising. Amazon pioneered the power of peer recommendations with the classic 5-star review system. Now sites such as Revoo.com have embraced this demand, setting out to create the *Which?* of the internet age. Syndicating their software to online retailers to enable the submission and recall of independent product feedback, they can also pull this data back into the Reevoo.com website to create a comprehensive database of reviews, and a destination portal in its own right.

ThisNext is one of our current favourite websites. It uses the simple idea that we are more likely to listen to our friends' views when purchasing. As a second-best option, we'll listen to a stranger who is similar to us in terms of demographics or outlook.

Pioneering yet retaining simplicity in its user interface, the site encourages people to submit products they like with the aim of creating a social shopping network where people explore, discover and rave about the hottest and most unique products on the web. By directly tapping into passions, they have managed to mobilise a community and create a potential new addiction.

Coolhunter is also a neat example of a trend-scouting blog that has activated its user base to help generate the site content. By tapping into their passions for identifying all things cool (with a fairly unrestrictive brief) this has helped create a loyal community. In turn, the accumulation of in-depth knowledge about this grouping, and the clear demographic profile it attracts, has enabled the website to develop many new commercial income streams, notably in online retail, trend consultancy and travel. With a readership that has snowballed in just a few short years since its inception in 2004 to something approaching 680,000 unique visitors per month, this site has mastered a powerful viral approach to promotion.

In a similar vein, Woot.com has prioritised

SUCCESSFUL MUSEUM RETAILING

community building over traditional e-commerce, in order to drive more sales. With a fascinating model, the site only sells one product per day, but has developed a highly devoted and active community around this principle. The site does not announce products beforehand, and takes an irreverent voice with copy often mocking the products and the customers. Users do their own research on the product and add it into the forums, including product reviews (positive and negative) and price comparisons. Site owner Matthew Shultz also records a daily podcast which briefly describes the item up for sale and includes a humorous song or skit.

Consumer development = audience development
KnockKnock is a stateside website pertaining to put the fun into functional (similar to MOO in the UK, who "love to print"). They ooze brand personality and are not afraid to be different as they recognise the role of marketing to clear segments. They are living testimony to the Seth Godin principle (bestselling author of *Tribes* and *Purple Cow*) that there is no such thing as the generic consumer beholden to the impact of disruptive TV advertising (the megaphone approach). By unleashing the passions of niche market segments, or the people that actually care about your product,

you are able to turn the megaphone around and attract through influencers. In their unique position, the brands of culture institutions need to be leaders rather than part of the herd – if they are to be heard! Standard is no longer good enough for today's consumer, they want bespoke (as standard).

Extending the reach of culture brands through retail broadens recognition, and widens the number of people interacting with the culture institution. More fundamentally, however, the short step from online consumer to offline visitor becomes apparent. In Madrid, Google and the Prado Museum have teamed up to allow web browsers to view 14 of the museum's works in striking detail through Google Earth. Google Spain director Javier Rodriguez Zapatero told the *International Herald Tribune* that the images now available on the Internet were 1,400 times clearer than what would be rendered with a 10-megapixel camera. "With Google Earth technology it is possible to enjoy these magnificent works in a way never previously possible, obtaining details impossible to appreciate through firsthand observation," he explained. His attitude to online engagement was just as telling, however. Nothing could replace the act of standing before a painting, or seeing it hung as part of a collection. "What we have here is a scientific level of detail," he said. "What we can access here is the body of the painting. But we cannot access its soul."

Global village

As the wonder of digital makes distance no object, every niche is now finding its devoted audience from the global melting pot. Smaller culture institutions in particular can thrive alongside their bigger cousins by adopting a specialised niche strategy. Before the 90s, if consumers didn't come within a certain radius of the culture institution, chances are they'd not be worth the marketing pounds. Now they're part of a niche – a potential new friend and customer, wherever they are.

Institutional members of niche communities are best placed to create an offer that truly "gets" their target market. If, as an institution, it makes your figurative hair stand on end, it's bound to do the same to your target market. Such is the beauty of chasing consumers in the Long Tail age: out there, somewhere, are consumers just like us. The mass market is now becoming a million mini-markets (see the way micro networks are emerging from the social networking phenomenon). The secret is in knowing which niche(s) we're an authoritative institutional member of, and finding the space where that community resides.

In this environment, a global outlook to

e-commerce is essential. 27.1% of total internet usage is in Europe but a massive 37.6% is in Asia and 17.5% in North America. In Asia, this is still only 15.3% of the total population compared to 48.1% in Europe and a huge 73.6% in North America[2]. Fresh on the heels of the one hundred dollar laptop is India's aspiration to build a laptop for only $7USD. The UK also has the most active online population in Europe, with the highest average number of daily visitors (21.8m), the highest usage days per month (21 per user), and the highest average time spent per month per user (34.4 hours)[3].

International demand for UK culture brands is riding high, and international brand extension through the retail channel offers a cost-efficient solution. In just a few months since launch, 20% of the traffic to CultureLabel.com is already coming from the US, thanks to the strong media profile through titles such as the Wall Street Journal. The logistics of international fulfilment become an essential consideration as globalised e-commerce capabilities develop, but third party infrastructures are now well-established for handling distribution at this level. On the front end, handling multiple currencies may add costs, but the returns for iconic UK brands are significant. Territory-specific content in the vein of BBC.com is also worth considering. On a regional level, and as an example of a visitor interface applying this thinking, Tate Online's integration of national with location-specific content is well worth reference.

Back to the starting point

In our overview and exploration of these four influences, we've deliberately focused on consumer trends rather than the nuts and bolts of SEO/PPC, onsite merchandising, digital marketing, analytics and so forth. Why? Because it's easy to slip into the dangerous territory of supply-led development at the expense of demand-led: the *How do we?* rather than the *Who wants it?* and *How do they want it?*

Build it and chances are they won't come in this case. Too often sites are developed without a clear audience in mind, and websites are built because everyone else has one, rather than to meet a specific demand. Each example explored above, and indeed the CultureLabel.com development experience, points to consumer-centricity as the only valid starting point. Understand your current and future consumers, and your site and e-commerce store develops in the context of a relationship.

74% of online shoppers willingly sign up to e-mail alerts from their favourite retailers. To get to this level of mutuality and emotional attachment requires clear consumer insight. Start with consumers, see what they're doing already, and explore how your cultural content – in this case digital or product-driven – can fit into their existing routines. Culture meeting consumers; the anchor upon which successful online culture retail must be built.

How culture can connect with consumers is also explored by the authors in *Intelligent Naivety: Commercial Opportunities for Museums and Culture Institutions*, 2009. You can also register for a free digital copy of the book at www.IntelligentNaivety.com[4].

1. *Source: IMRG*

2. *Source: Miniwatts Marketing Group, 2008*

3. *Source: comScore*

4. *Intelligent Naivety is a CultureLabel production supported by the MLA Council as part of the Entrepreneurial Museum project.*

ALIVE TO CHANGE

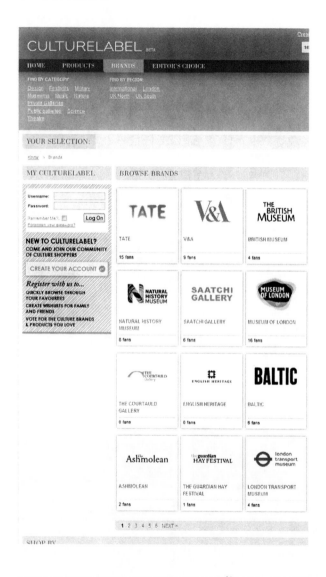

"FINGERS" KINETIC SCULPTURE BY NIK RAMAGE
FOR LAIKINGLAND

BOB AND ROBERTA SMITH BLOCKS FOR TATE

MORE IMAGES: WWW.MUSEUMSETC.COM/?PAGE_ID=1378

13

A Path to the Future

AUNDREA HOLLINGTON

Head of Retail Projects

Historic Scotland

Retail is a vital resource in the heritage and museums sector – a way to raise much-needed revenue while adding to the visitor experience.

Like many organisations, Historic Scotland cannot rely on the public purse to provide all the resources it needs for the upkeep of properties, staff pay and to fund the many other projects it wants to undertake.

There's only so much that can be done with ticket prices – most of our sites are free but 68 charge an admission price – as a proper balance has to be achieved between public access and the need to generate income. Retail is in the special position of providing an avenue for earning money without running the risk of deterring visitors.

This is a hugely important consideration given the economic climate when people are having to think very hard before taking days out, short breaks or decide on holiday destinations.

Fortunately for us, this has all happened at a time when we have already spent several years developing our retail services so they are sharply focused and efficient. As such we have become leaders in areas like organising product promotions.

At the same time we have taken, and continue to take, huge strides in making sure the product ranges in our 75 retail outlets (a number of sites have multiple retail outlets) reflect the character of the site and provide what our customers want.

This is no straightforward task as our estate consists of an eclectic mix of castles, abbeys, prehistoric settlements and tombs, plus industrial sites including a distillery and an eighteenth century cotton mill complex. They vary from world famous attractions like Edinburgh Castle, right in the heart of a great European capital city, to a simple thatch-roofed Victorian blackhouse set amidst the wild beauties of the Western Isles.

At the same time our outlets, which range from relatively spacious shops to wooden cabins, and small areas within visitor centres and ticket offices, provide a mixed bag of places in which to lay out our wares.

What we have done is had a top-to-toe rethink of every aspect of our retailing.

The most obvious outward sign of this was to streamline what we sell by creating a series of product ranges that accurately reflect the character of our attractions. Themes include kings, queens (and naturally princes and princesses), castles, abbeys, banqueting, Celtic and much more.

More clarity has meant cutting the clutter as we have stripped out under-performing items and, in some cases, opened up much-needed extra space to improve the atmosphere of an outlet.

It's a truism I repeat to myself every time I'm tempted to add something extra into a retail area, less really is more.

Having ranges has also allowed us to become much better at monitoring sales. Nowadays, they are refreshed every year by reducing or removing items that don't sell and introducing something new.

And experimentation has become important. Our change of approach has made us more imaginative and creative. A particular pleasure has been the chance to work with talented young artists, like Alice Druit. Her cards were being sold at Edinburgh Castle and we really took to the designs, so commissioned her to produce a whole series of fun cartoon illustrations in the *Castles* and *Cathedrals* ranges. They have been used on a range of products from mugs to notebooks to bookmarks and certain products in the Castle-theme in particular have been a big hit.

No two Historic Scotland properties are alike and so we have recognised that their retail offerings should also be distinctive.

This has meant ensuring that there are attractive, often inexpensive, site-specific goods on offer like mugs, postcards and bookmarks, perhaps featuring an historic image of the site.

These little mementoes are the things, just like crested china in the early twentieth century or little felt pennants printed with the names of seaside resorts, that are often taken home and treasured for years.

Despite the individuality of each site, we have also had to recognise that there may be several Historic Scotland properties in the same area. Indeed, the Scottish Borders are famed for their great medieval abbeys like Dryburgh, Melrose and Jedburgh. We make sure that visitors taking in several properties in a day, or weekend, are not faced with an identical range of goods.

We are continually striving to improve and innovate on the administrative side of our business as well as introducing what we call the *shop-in-a-box* system for a number of our smaller sites.

In the past, all requests for extra stock regardless of the size of the property had to come through our Edinburgh headquarters. From this year, because these outlets know just what they should be stocking and in what quantities, their repeat orders will be handled directly by the warehouse and distribution staff and whatever they need will be boxed up and sent off. This is shortening the supply chain, cutting costs, reducing red tape and freeing up staff time among my small central team to concentrate on other projects.

We are also doing more to empower staff on-site – the people who often have years of insight and expertise about the sort of people who come through our sites and what they buy. As a result we have established a network of retail champions, staff who can take the initiative in promoting the shop at their site.

At the same time we are encouraging staff to become decision makers by doing things like carrying out impromptu promotions. So nowadays if things are a little slack, they can fish out a bottle of what their sales reports and experience tells them is a top-selling whisky or liqueur and offer tastings.

We also have a promotional calendar for Edinburgh and Stirling castles which sees suppliers send in their own staff to do something a little more formal through the height of the season. Both approaches work well.

We are increasingly using special offers on everything from quality teas, shortbreads and even collectables like children's model knights in armour.

Times might be tough but people still love a bargain and we are becoming as commercially-minded as anyone on the High Street to make sure they find good deals when they shop with us.

So, while visitor figures for 2008-09 across the heritage sector fell, our retail outlets have fared pretty well. Being proactive has been critical and we are fully aware that it's an ongoing process. But, going forward, a key development will be to reorganise in a way that recognises that just as the history of each site is different, so is its retail potential.

That has led us to look at dividing them up into three categories: commercial sites, development sites and community sites. The names are largely self-explanatory but the effect will be invaluable in allowing us to set objectives and decide how to achieve them.

In some cases, the aim is to provide suitable and appealing products for attractions which have modest numbers of visitors. In others, like Iona Abbey, we have been able to identify that more can be achieved and by designating them as Development Sites we are making sure this gets discussed and done.

Then there is the big reality that certain sites, like Edinburgh and Stirling castles with about 1.6 million visitors a year between them, have far more potential customers than others.

Looking at the numbers and potential earnings in this way has not, however, distracted us from the recognition that we are part of a public body dedicated to promoting the access and enjoyment of our national heritage. In fact it is all part and parcel of pursuing those wider goals, not just by raising funding but in helping determine what we sell.

At the most obvious level there are the official souvenir guidebooks, a mainstay of many Community Site outlets. Our colleagues in the Interpretation Unit, with whom we work very closely, have been doing a great job of updating these to make them more accessible and appealing, helping improve sales, and doing their bit to modernise the image of Historic Scotland.

Then there are the many other books, including lots to fire up young imaginations.

One of the most promising advances we have made is in strengthening the links between people in different departments within our own organisation.

So now when there is a new project underway we all work together from the start, pooling our expertise.

Right now that is happening with the Stirling Castle Palace project. This is a £12 million scheme to return the royal palace within the castle to how it may have looked when it was brand new in the mid-sixteenth century. Those were the days when the four-poster bed was the very latest in upper-class continental chic.

Its walls will be graced by a series of huge hand-woven tapestries, of which four are complete, which tell the popular medieval tale of the Hunt of the Unicorn. Each time a new one comes off the loom we use it as the basis for items in our popular Tapestries Range. These are quality products including fine bone china and reproduction tapestries.

Later this year we will start developing other lines ready for the reopening of the palace in 2011-12. One likely source of inspiration will be the Stirling Heads, huge metre-wide carved oak medallions which once decorated the ceilings of some of the most important chambers in the palace. They feature kings, queens, emperors and classical heroes. Each would have been familiar to famous figures like Mary, Queen of Scots and James VI and I, for whom the palace was an important residence.

Being guided through the palace by costumed performers is likely to be quite an experience and we want to make sure that we go beyond the obvious in coming up with imaginative goods that people can take away as gifts or keepsakes.

We also try to look outwards.

Locally-produced crafts are integrated into the ranges at a variety of sites like Iona Abbey and Maeshowe and Skara Brae in Orkney. In each case, we add to the character of the goods, and hopefully to the sales of the producer, by attaching cards with details about them and their work.

One thing that is becoming increasingly clear is that we can never afford to stand still. Historic Scotland, and Scotland itself, is competing on a local, national and international level to bring in visitors and make sure they have such a good time they become our ambassadors when they go home.

Retail has a vital role to play in this. So this year we will be doing all we can to build and strengthen our position. This will partly be done by carrying out extensive market research to get a clearer picture of what customers want. In doing so we are recognising that old realities are changing, among them the importance of the American market.

The fact that Edinburgh Castle's Official Souvenir Guide Books now include Gaelic, Russian and Chinese language versions says a great deal.

The fundamental lesson I hope we have learned, and the common thread that runs through all the changes we have made, is the need to be alive to change. From this position we can create retail opportunities that ensure we raise vital revenue and that our visitors will leave with something more than just memories.

Case study: Edinburgh Castle

Listening to what visitors say led Historic Scotland off in a quite unexpected direction at Edinburgh Castle.

A far-reaching project in 2008 saw a complete rebranding exercise for what is Scotland's premier paid-for visitor attraction. Part of the exercise involved the creation of stylish new uniforms using a specially designed and highly attractive Edinburgh Castle tartan in red and black. The public liked the uniforms and started asking for them. So now our shops at the castle are selling ties, scarves and Tam o' Shanter hats in our new tartan.

Likewise Historic Scotland has tried to be imaginative about how it responded to the new brand image, which includes an impressive Defender of the Nation lion logo. The image reworks the idea of the castle standing high on its volcanic rock into a crown on the head of a roaring lion with flowing mane. It is striking, simple and easily reproduced for use on all sorts of items.

The result is an extensive Edinburgh Castle Logo Range of items that make excellent mementoes for adults and older children. But the Retail Department also wanted something that younger children would like. So they worked with Emma Dodd, whose cute pictures of domestic moggies had been spotted in books, and asked her if she'd like to try her hand at a rather larger cat.

The result is a delight: friendly and fun, and very much a character in his own right. So much so that he has been nicknamed Ruairidh – or Rory for those not familiar with Scottish spellings. In July 2009 the

Roary range was launched and our loveable lion now appears on T-shirts, wellington boots, water bottles, lunch boxes, stationery products and a rather cute and cuddly soft toy.

Overall, the castle project, which has included a multi-million pound visitor reception area, website and online ticketing, has demonstrated the value of stepping outside organisational roles and looking at things from the visitors' perspective.

That meant recognising that while the castle is very much a part of the Historic Scotland portfolio, to the public it has an iconic status and identity entirely separate from who runs the place.

This freed up the organisation to create a resonant brand which carries across everything from publicity material to retail goods. Just as important is that it acts as a spur rather than a brake on creativity, providing the chance to respond to customer demand and to be imaginative over the development of new products.

Case study: Stanley Mills
The Stanley Mills project was something quite new for Historic Scotland. It involved taking parts of a once-magnificent eighteenth century cotton mill complex on the banks of the River Tay, near Perth, and turning it into a hi-tech education and visitor centre full of

interactive exhibits and displays.

As a relatively young organisation, established in 1991, most of Historic Scotland's properties were already in state care and open to the public. This was one of the first opportunities to develop an attraction from scratch. The organisation took an integrated approach to its development, ensuring that retail needs were integral to the planning and not an afterthought.

When the visitor centre opened, at Easter 2008, it was welcomed with excellent publicity. Rather than having a separate shop, the decision had been made to have a sales and ticketing area inside the front entrance. The effect is that the shape of the original mill space has not been compromised and that there is lots to look at and enjoy from the moment the doors open.

The retail department was closely involved with the overall branding of Stanley Mills. This was a vital part of the project which involved trying to capture the essence of a water mill complex that had led Scotland's charge into the industrial revolution, surviving 200 years before dwindling into dereliction in the 1980s.

The branding was eventually refined into four core ideas: people, place, power and products. Historic Scotland worked with external consultants to come up with a design that would capture these themes and that could be used on everything from signage and leaflets to letterheads and, of course, merchandise.

The result is a highly distinctive image of interconnected cogs which was inspired by the wonderfully engineered mechanism that operated the sluice gates controlling the flow of water from the lades to the mills. It incorporates ideas about history and power and contrasts the fluid softness of water with the hardness of the metal. Just as important is that it is not the sort of thing that will date quickly – an important consideration for merchandising.

The whole exercise was a success. Stanley exceeded its first season visitor targets by a mile and there are now Stanley Mills branded mugs, tea towels and much more. What was lacking was the human side. This was a place where Perthshire peasant farmers thrown off their land in the Highland Clearances had sought a new life. And during the eighteenth and nineteenth centuries the mills had made extensive use of child labour. It was also a place which had provided a fresh start for substantial numbers of Italians escaping poverty in the twentieth century – including some escaping the grim aftermath of World War II.

A well-known multilingual poet, Aonghas MacNeacail, was commissioned to write a series of poems about life at the mills in the three tongues most common among the workforce – English, Scots and

Gaelic. These now appear on the walls in a top-floor area where there are also audio-visual exhibits highlighting moments from workers' lives. The poet's words now also appear on products such as bookmarks.

Another way of reflecting the human side of Stanley into the product range was made possible by the discovery of a fantastic group shot of the workers gathered outside the mills in the 1880s. The picture has a prominent place inside the visitor centre and has also been used on a postcard, mug and notebook. As such it has played an important role in the job of creating a clear brand identity for the centre.

Overall, the integrated approach taken to the site's development has ensured that there is a sense of coherence in every aspect of the visitor experience at Stanley Mills. A mark of its success is that VisitScotland awarded it five star status – marking it out as a world class attraction – within months of the official opening.

MORE IMAGES: WWW.MUSEUMSETC.COM/?PAGE _ ID=1378

14

New Product Development

SUE TOWNSEND

Managing Director

Gifted In Design Limited

In today's society it is virtually impossible to navigate the day without coming into contact with the power of brands and the underlying promises that the brands seek to deliver. Billions of dollars are spent worldwide on marketing and advertising to reinforce key brand messages and values, or even to devalue a competitor's offer. But all with the common goal of selling you a product or a service and securing your future purchase loyalty.

There is a commonality to successful brands. They all, first and foremost, deliver a fantastic product which is then maximised through great branding, marketing and most importantly multichannel retailing. Good retailers understand that their products are the stars of the show and will be asking themselves the following questions about their required retail environments:

- what it is they are trying to say and communicate to their desired customers about their brand;
- and how do they want to say it, in what tone of voice?

When you walk into an Apple store you are immediately under no illusion that you have arrived in technology heaven: modern, bright and with attentive retail associates to help navigate even the biggest technology phobic. You are positively encouraged to touch and interact with the products, you will be seduced with their ease-of-use and all that they can do to enhance your life. This retail experience works on every sensory level.

BMW showrooms, the homes of the ultimate driving machines, sell you a lifestyle: sit for hours on plump cushioned sofas drinking copious cups of coffee whilst building your ultimate driving machine on a computer screen. Matching your leather seats with walnut or black trims, holding a glossy metallic colour chip in your hand, debating on how badly you need heated front seats for the cold, or more importantly rear parking sensors so you never have to really think whilst parking again. Ultimately, these brands deliver their stories because the products match and over-deliver against the promises made in the marketing and retail environments.

In the case of both these brands, product creation came first and they then developed into the Superbrands we know and recognise today. This is not always the case, with strong product brands being created thanks to an ability to diversify into new markets based on the strengths of one division, or on a desire to satisfy customer requests. You need only look at the power of "celebrity" and the numerous products, product collections and product endorsements born out of their original fame and talent which allows us to trust, desire and buy into a piece of their lives through their products. If their fans wear their perfume, they are sharing in their lifestyle and their unique point of view; by buying and wearing a concert t-shirt they are attaching themselves to that moment of enjoyment and celebrating their shared experience. Although everyone will have their own celebrity in mind whilst reading this piece, we need look no further than one of our most infamous exports - the Beckhams - to see this trend in full effect across the world. And it is not just in celebrity that we see such retailing diversification; it is evidenced across numerous businesses. Richard Branson's Virgin group began life as a record store and expanded across the music business, moved into the airline and holiday space and continued to diversify from trains, to finance and money and even to his own cola, if maybe not as successfully. Because the customer aligned with the Virgin core values and philosophies, this allowed the brand to be harnessed into these diverse businesses and however strange they may have looked on paper it all worked! It is with these brands that museums find their greatest alignment and opportunity for growth. Museums - their organisations and their galleries - already have all the makings of potential successful retail brands; by the very nature of their existence they are brimming over with uniqueness and are reaching a regular dedicated audience that will willingly convert to being a purchasing customer.

Harnessing your brand for product development
Museums invest heavily in creating the right environment for their collections, placing the displays in context so their stories can be told from their historical perspective. Increasingly interactive, the visit experience combines education and research with the intention of inspiring and sending the visitor away thinking differently, finding new connections with everyday life. Product, product collections and retail shops should be a natural extension of these values and philosophies.

But, all too often, this is the part of the visitor experience that is devalued - being treated with slight contempt due to its obvious commercial nature or its perceived lack of academic credibility. Yet this is the piece of the visit that the customer takes away with them and keeps as a constant memory and memento of this important time spent. I have heard product called *sidelines, nic nacs, bits and pieces* and all manner of other derogatory terminology. So the first step on this product journey is to *be as passionate about your product as you are about your exhibits and collections.*

Your second step is *preparation* - whether using the skills of a product design agency or whether managing the process in-house: preparation is key. Here are a few questions that should be worked through in advance of designing a single product.

Do you have brand guidelines? Brand guidelines form the basis of your product brand map. They ensure that you not only use the right colour palettes and tone of voice to reflect your museum, but they support any product development and ensure that all the product items created are suitable for your organisation. Use product examples to test your product map. Ask yourself at what point does a product become damaging to, rather than a positive addition to, your brand. This might involve the country and circumstances in which the product is being produced.

Whilst working on the Blackwell product map we had to ensure that the brand leveraged its heritage and diverse customer age and demographic whilst recognising the need to sell to the younger student generation - without alienating the academic credibility the brand was built on. Moving this brand away from its patronising and inappropriate "sex, drugs and rock-and-roll" student product position to one of wit, eloquence, intelligence and being current, at its simplest involved removed lines such as vodka shot glasses and replacing them with artist product work such as that of Stephen Appleby.

What are the unique features of your museum and its collections? This may seem like an obvious question but it never does any harm to reflect on what makes you special. This may take the form of an overall theme or statement of being, or it could be a combination of different exhibits and collections. For instance, if we were to review the special features of the Wellcome Collection we could include *medical, incurably curious, DNA double helix, Jelly man 3...*

What are your most popular exhibits and why? You will know which exhibits, collections or single pieces draw the most attention from your audiences. You should also list the reasons why this is the case. This will help you with the conversion to potential product. For instance, if it is the exhibit's sheer size you are unlikely to be able to replicate this exactly, but by a change of product format you could provide the same effect, perhaps by using the medium of film.

What other resources are available to you in your archives? You probably have a wealth of unexplored materials just waiting to be discovered and converted. This will be a rich source of brand collateral for a new and exciting offer and can ensure that you always have the opportunity to continue to grow and diversify your ranges.

Why do people come to visit you rather than another museum? It was Walt Disney who said ,"You can design and create and build the most wonderful place in the world, but it takes people to make the dream a reality." Although once again seemingly obvious, this part of the process is sometimes too readily taken for granted. Take out a small amount of time to quickly check your assumptions. Bypassing this stage is a high risk. Take the opportunity to speak to your visitors; set up small focus groups; ask your visitors to complete quick exit surveys about what they enjoyed about their visit and why they would recommend you to their family and friends; and whether you would capture that all-important return visit or membership to your organisation? Once answered, you will have the basis of your materials.

What other activities and exhibits happen within your museum? Most run exceptional programmes of specifically targeted and themed new exhibits, talks and tours. These should be taken into consideration as they invariably attract good attendances and can provide your membership with the opportunity to make repeat visits and, of course, they present the opportunity to produce exhibit-centric products.

Sales performances by line? Against previous years? By trading channel? If you are already trading a product offer it is absolutely essential you monitor and review individual product performances and monitor sales results. It was once famously said that doing the same thing achieves the same results. This analysis should give you a good insight into what works for your business and where the future opportunities lie.

No masterpiece was ever created by a lazy artist. Salvador Dali.

Step Three in the process is to *Know your customer.* It is important to have a very clear idea of who your current customers are and in what proportion they make up your attendance figures. This will ensure you create collections tuned to the right audience. If your audience is predominantly schools, you should prioritise and focus on providing a product collection tailored to meet their age ranges and likely available budget, rather than an expensive signature collection which may look fantastic in the shop but create few sales. At this point it would be wise to invest in spending some time with the keepers of the knowledge of the business - the employee team. By engaging the team you will ensure you capture all the on-the-ground knowledge - from customer commentary, to regular requests. These sessions are likely to break up some of the myths and legends that always surround businesses: "We don't do that because..." "That will never work for us..." Without jumping to too many assumptions it is likely that your customer base will include a combination of *general tourist/visitor attraction customers* looking for a special memento to remember their visit by, or to give as a gift to a loved one. *Special exhibition customers* - this category would include your schools tours and destination exhibition traffic - who are much more targeted with their visit and are very likely to return if they enjoy their initial experience. *Members or Friends* who are much more expert in their positioning and relationship with your organisation, who will be regular attenders and real supporters and are likely to be looking to nurture a deeper relationship with your brand and its products.

Step Four: *Know your competition*. Although it is likely you are unique in your offer, you will at some point be fighting for the same customer. Conducting a SWOT (strengths, weaknesses, opportunities and threats) analysis on your competitors will ensure you not only learn from your competitors' product offers, how they are put together, their pricing architecture, and their product mix, but it could stop you repeating the same mistakes. Look at all trading channels for competition as there will be as many competitors online and within the direct mail sectors.

This work may take time, but once completed, all the preparation work undertaken by you or your agency should give you a complete and lasting foundation on which to create your product collections. It should also ensure you minimise costly mistakes.

So how do you go about choosing product and design agencies? Whilst it is definitely worthwhile investing in a quality product agency, do ensure they meet the following criteria and can deliver the following requirements.

Do they have a good history of product design - not just marketing design - as product design involves both 2D and 3D design. Take references from previous clients and let them show you samples and product produced for other clients so you have an idea of the quality of their work.

Do they understand your sector? It isn't necessarily essential that they have previously worked in your sector, as sometimes a fresh perspective can be valuable, but it is essential they do not base all of their knowledge on other product sectors.

Where possible they should have the ability to deliver the actual product not just the design.

This demonstrates that the agency understands manufacturing, and designs with materials and sourcing quantities in mind - which will undoubtedly save your budget.

If they are sourcing overseas, can they demonstrate a good knowledge of their supply chain, especially the credentials and operating practices of their factories? Many agencies source from third parties themselves and cannot demonstrate the necessary knowledge of who you could ultimately be conducting business with.

Ensure that when they accept the brief they have accounted for all the necessary preparatory work suggested earlier and can show a solid grasp of your brand before they begin to develop product scamps. This could and should be incorporated into a pitch document if you are interviewing more than one agency for the role.

Ensure they engage you in the process every step of the way, showing you the development of the product scamps and allowing you to sign off pre-production samples to ensure you like the quality and direction the product has taken.

Agree a budget in advance for the work being undertaken.

Have they thought about how you are going to actually sell the product? At what price point? What the packaging strategy is? What fixturing would work best to maximise the display of the selected product? Can they offer any assistance in the visual merchandising of the product? Do they constantly have your customer at the front of their minds? Do you like them? Will they be good to work with?

If you think it's expensive to hire a professional to the job, wait until you hire an amateur. Red Adair.

The alternative to using the skills of a quality agency - depending on your appetite for control, your anticipated turnover and your future growth strategy - is to consider recruiting your own internal buyer. I have worked in the retail sector for over twenty years and have operated in both retail front-of-house and behind-the-scenes in buying and marketing, but the key to all successful organisations remains the same: *Your people are your greatest asset and most valuable commodity.* Good buyers with international sourcing experience are worth their weight in gold.

If I was looking for a buyer today, I would be looking for the following attributes and experience:

· An exceptional understanding of factory processes, product component development and product development. The understanding of all of the key components in making up the products is key to the factory's achieving your required quality and pricing.

- Experience across the retail channel, although not essential, is invaluable. The best buyers have had experience directly with the customer, have worked on the sales floor and have gained a good understanding of the mechanics of managing product from goods-in and stockrooms to visual merchandising on the sales floor. They will have also had direct contact with the supply chain, have a good knowledge of overseas agents and of working direct with factories.

- Excellent communication skills as they are crucial for managing the internal and external customer on all issues relating the product, such as marketing.

- They must be able to build excellent relationships and partnerships, as they will be continually receiving and asking for feedback as well as negotiating on your behalf. To give you a broad product range they will need not only to forge relationships within the supply chain but likely with other product brands for potential concessions and product developments.

- Good mathematical and budgeting skills. This is essential to the role since a good buyer spends much time managing sales, margins, stockturns and mark downs to ensure you maximise sales and profit.
- An excellent understanding of your brand and a willingness to work within your guidelines. Although all good buyers will be able to create products and be innovative in their approach, they should never be buying for themselves and their own taste but should always remain firmly rooted in your brand map – so strong opinions softly held!
- A can-do attitude with the *right product, right place, right time* as the end goal to be achieved.

With either a good buyer or a good agency in place, you are now in a position to begin creating your product collections. My last pieces of advice are to buy in limited quantities at first until you have found your market - you can always increase your stocks with a replenishment run. And never to be afraid to develop something new. As Henry Ford said, "If I'd asked people what they wanted they would have said a faster horse!"

Unprovided with original learning, unformed in the habits of thinking, unskilled in the arts of composition, I resolved to **write** a book.

Edward Gibbon

BLACKWELL

MORE IMAGES: WWW.MUSEUMSETC.COM/?PAGE_ID=1378

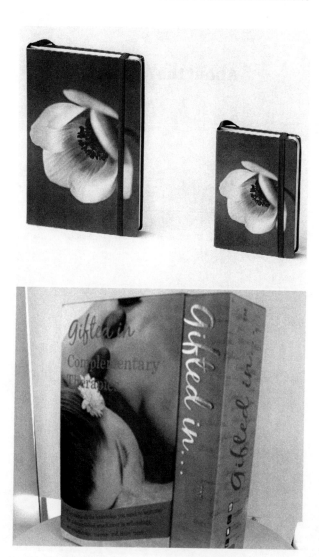

15

About the Authors

Louisa Adkins is Compton Verney's Commercial Manager. Before joining the organisation in 2004 she worked in high street and museum retail. Compton Verney is a comparatively new art gallery set in a Robert Adam mansion house where she is responsible for all aspects of the retail and admissions functions, from selling tickets and guidebooks to managing EPoS and ticket processing systems, as well as visual merchandising, buying and product development.

Iain Betterton has been the Commercial Manager at Dulwich Picture Gallery since June 2004. After graduating from the University of Hull in 1996, he joined Direct Shopping Ltd based in Putney where he oversaw the production of five annual copies of the mail order gift catalogue *Presents Direct*, sister publication to *Cucina Direct*. In 2003, a deviation in his career path took him *Around the World on £20 a Day* for the Saturday Telegraph. He then joined Memorisethis.com, a leading gift, gadget and experiences website as Head of Retail, producing a successful mail order catalogue.

Caroline Brown began her retail career as a sales assistant with Oddbins Wine Merchants and left, 16 years later, as the Regional Sales Manager for the largest area in the company. She moved to the National

Maritime Museum as Head of Retail in 2005, and now, as Head of Commerce, her role encompasses retail, catering, commercial events and filming, publishing, picture library, photo studio and licensing .

Kate Bull is one of the UK's leading retail strategists. Her credentials extend across all aspects of retailing, both in the UK and overseas. From franchise development and purchasing to business strategy and employee engagement, she has extensive experience in helping clients shape and deliver the right customer and employee retail strategy.

Simon Cronshaw is a co-founder of CultureLabel and leads on the development of practical tools for developing e-commerce and digital marketing for culture institutions. Most recently, he oversaw *Release1.0*, an international design competition for artists to develop new culture merchandise for sale at the ICA, with other partners including Warp Records and the London Design Festival. He comes from a background in research and consumer insight, having recently finished as Head of the Research Unit at Arts & Business where he commissioned work from international luminaries such as Pine and Gilmore. His main interest is in the changing nature of cultural consumption, as well as bespoke business strategies for creative and cultural businesses. Simon specialises in trend/market analysis, forecasting and strategic/tactical planning for enterprises. He possesses a strong track record in devising positioning and revenue strategies for a wide range of culture institution clients.

Jeremy Ensor currently heads up the Natural History Museum's Retail and Licensing businesses, which he and his team have developed and grown successfully over the last four years. Prior to this, he worked for Heal's for seven years as a Store Manager and Project Manager opening new department stores nationwide. He started his retail career in Selfridges, where he spent seven years in various Buying and Sales Management roles.o

Aundrea Hollington is Head of Retail Projects at Historic Scotland, based in Edinburgh. She joined the organisation in 1996 as Retail Buying & Display Controller and took on the new role as Head of Retail Projects in 2009. Historic Scotland is the largest operator of paid-for visitor attractions in Scotland and the Retail Department is responsible for a chain of retail shops, including Edinburgh, Stirling and Urquhart

Castle. Before joining the Scottish Government Agency she worked in the private sector as a buyer and product development executive for Avon Cosmetics Ltd and before that was a buyer in the retail clothing sector with the George Davies Partnership.

Gregory Krum is an artist, sometime curator and the Director of Retail at the Cooper-Hewitt, National Design Museum in New York City. He studied Biology, Sculpture and Design and has a Master's degree in Photography. He was the first product manager at the New York design store *moss* and has worked in Beijing organizing a United Nations conference. He co-curated an art show in the language of a pop-up retail store with the Kantor/Feuer gallery in New York and is currently curating a fashion exhibition on the label *Rodarte* which opens at the Cooper-Hewitt in early 2010. His photographs have been shown nationally and can often be found at the Jen Bekman gallery in New York. He divides his time between New York and Hong Kong.

Nuala McGourty is Retail Director at Royal Collection Enterprises. Prior to that, she spent seven years with M&S, starting as a Management Trainee and progressing through procurement and merchandising on both foods and textiles. A move into fashion at Coats Patons followed, covering cloth buying, manufacturing and the merchandising of 130 Country Casuals shops, before becoming Purchasing and Distribution Director of Jaeger Ladieswear. Further spells at board level in fashion, menswear and lingerie environments followed, before she joined Royal Collection Enterprises in 1998.

Adam Thow is Head of Retail and Buying at Southbank Centre in London, a 21-acre site on the banks of the Thames that includes the Hayward Gallery, Royal Festival Hall, Queen Elizabeth Hall and a diverse artistic and commercial offering. He has previously worked in buying roles for the Natural History Museum and Tussauds Group (now Merlin Entertainments) in addition to purchasing and management roles in the promotional marketing sector.

Sue Townsend is Managing Director of Gifted In Design Limited. Voted *Everywoman's Director of the Year 2008*, she worked in retail operations, buying and marketing prior to setting up her own product agency. Her most recent retail role was as Commercial Director for Blackwell, where she not only successfully fully implemented a complete new product division but was instrumental in the team's being awarded *Retail Chain of the Year* and *Bookselling Company of the Year.*

Peter Tullin is a co-founder of CultureLabel, the first online portal for the products of leading museums and galleries worldwide. He is also the editor of IntelligentNaivety.com, a blog exploring the connection between culture and consumers, as well as commercial opportunities for culture institutions. Previously, as National Account Director at Arts & Business, he was responsible for developing and maintaining relationships with FTSE and multinational commercial clients. He has negotiated innovative, high profile culture-commerce collaborations with clients such as Ballymore Properties, BP, GSK, Microsoft, JTI and Stagecoach, and more recently has been helping A&B with commercialisation strategies and a major new capital project with a leading property developer, creating a new international centre of creativity. Peter is a regular speaker on the subject of business viability and cultural entrepreneurship at academic institutions and at sector conferences.

Michael Walton Michael Walton is Head of Trading at London Transport Museum, a division of Transport for London, where he has worked for nearly 30 years driving the development of one of London's best museum shops. With a background in advertising, he has worked on most commercial initiatives at London Transport Museum, including as a member of the Project Team for the 2007 Museum Rebuild. In addition to his involvement in a number of key Transport for London investment and event projects, he developed the first main Arts Strategy at Transport for London, and continues to commission artworks for Transport for London use. He is a frequent speaker at cultural sector and higher education conferences, and as a notable expert on commercial poster, retail and public transport design, is a regular media contributor. Current major projects include development and launch of a new integrated LTM/TfL commercial website, the creation of new business models and partners and the development and implementation of sophisticated print to order services for both organisations.

Michael Whitworth is Head of Commercial Operations at Manchester Museum. A graduate of Warwick University, he has had many years of experience in the retail sector, beginning his career with WHSmith before becoming a training branch manager with Royal Doulton UK. In 1997 he moved to Manchester Museum. He has a particular interest in proving the financial viability of fair trade, and sits on the University of Manchester Fair Trade Steering Group.

Also from MuseumsEtc

Inspiring Action: Museums and Social Change

Fifteen leading museum and gallery professionals contribute inspiring, practical essays on the ways in which their institutions are responding to the new social challenges of the twenty-first century.

Drawing on pioneering international experience from the UK, USA, Australia and Africa, these experienced professionals explore the theory and the practice of building social inclusion in museum and gallery programmes.

Contributors include: Ronna Tulgan-Ostheimer, Clarke Art Institute; Manon Parry, National Library of Medicine; Gabriela Salgado, Tate Modern; Katy Archer, NCCL Galleries of Justice; Peter Armstrong, Royal Armouries; Keith Cima, Tower of London; Olivia Guntarik, RMIT University; Elizabeth Wood, IUPUI School of Education; Gareth Knapman, Museum Victoria; Jennifer Scott, Weeksville Heritage; Susan Ghosh, Dulwich Picture Gallery; Jo Woolley, MLA; Marcia Zerivitz, Jewish Museum of Florida; Carol Brown, University of KwaZulu-Natal; Eithne Nightingale, V&A Museum.

ISBN: 978-0-9561943-1-2
Order online from www.museumsetc.com

Creating Bonds: Marketing Museums

Marketing professionals working in and with museums and galleries throughout the UK, USA and beyond, share their latest insights and experiences of involving and speaking to a wide range of constituencies. Their practical, insightful essays span the development and management of the museum brand; successful marketing initiatives within both the small museum and the large national museum environment; and the ways in which specific market sectors - both young and old - can be effectively targeted.

Contributors include: Amy Nelson, University of Kentucky Art Museum; Aundrea Hollington, Historic Scotland; Adam Lumb, Museums Sheffield; Bruno Bahunek, Museum of Contemporary Art, Zagreb; Claire Ingham, London Transport Museum; Kate Knowles, Dulwich Picture Gallery; Danielle Chidlow, National Gallery; Margot Wallace, Columbia College; Rachel Collins, Wellcome Collection; Sian Walters, National Museum Wales; Gina Koutsika, Tate; Alex Gates, North Berrien Historical Museum.

ISBN: 978-0-9561943-1-2
Order online from www.museumsetc.com

Rethinking Learning: Museums and Young People

Practical, inspirational case studies from senior museum and gallery professionals from Europe and the USA clearly demonstrate the way in which imaginative, responsive services for children and young people can have a transformational effect on the museum and its visitor profile as a whole.

Authors recount how, for example – as a direct result of their focus on young people – attendance has increased by 60% in three years; membership has reached record levels; and repeat visits have grown from 30% to 50%. Many of the environments in which these services operate are particularly challenging: city areas where 160 different languages are spoken; a remote location whose typical visitor has to travel 80 miles; the museum which targets children with challenging physical, mental or behavioural needs.

This is an essential book not only for those working with children and young people, but for those in any way concerned with museum and gallery policy, strategy, marketing and growth.

ISBN: 978-0-9561943-0-5
Order online from www.museumsetc.com

The Power of the Object:
Museums and World War II

In this important new book, based on a conference held by the National Museum of Denmark, international museum professionals deal with the key issues affecting all history museums, using as the basis for their insights the interpretation by museums of World War II.

Among the many issues the contributors address are:

- How best can abstractions like cause, effect and other ideas be interpreted through objects?
- Just how is the role of objects within museums changing?
- How should we respond when increasingly visitors no longer accept the curator's choice of objects and their interpretation?
- How can museums deal effectively with controversial historical issues?

These essays explore how history museums can help explain and interpret the thinking of past generations, as well as their material culture.

ISBN: 978-0-9561943-4-3
Order online from www.museumsetc.com

Twitter for Museums

There are books about how to use Twitter, but none about how best museums and galleries, large and small, can – and are – using the social media platform, Twitter, to involve their very diverse communities. This book aims to remedy this situation.

Drawing on the experience of leading users of Twitter throughout the world, the book both explains how to use Twitter, and demonstrates best practice through a series of in-depth case studies.

The Twitter platform has itself been used extensively in the development of the book, and the publication will be available as a traditional paperback, as well as in eBook format, and will link to online resources to allow frequent updating.

Available: Spring 2010

Narratives of Community and Hope: Museums and Ethnicity

Edited by Dr Olivia Guntarik, RMIT University, Melbourne, Australia

This forthcoming book will examine museum approaches to the representation of ethnic minorities. A series of essays will discuss the forms of cultural participation in the museum as a narrative and interpretative space. We aim to feature essays on the ways ethnic communities help to articulate our interests in marginal voices in historiography and cross-cultural forms of representation.

The book will be oriented towards outlining and drawing together the current insights and concerns of academic researchers and museum professionals, including members of ethnic community groups who have been involved in creating their own narratives in museum displays and exhibitions.

Available: Spring 2010

The Science Exhibition:
Curation, Design, Communication

Edited by Dr Anastasia Filippoupoliti
Museologist and Historian of Science,
Democritus University of Thrace, Greece

This forthcoming book will explore three related themes in relation to science exhibitions in museums: the processes involved in developing new science exhibitions in and for museums; the issues involved in transforming scientific ideas or events into exhibitions; the challenges faced by museums in communicating science to a wide audience.

We are particularly interested in new, innovative and successful initiatives in this field.

Much has been written about the difficulties of disseminating science to the public through a variety of new and traditional media. It is, indeed, a complex subject to tackle in the exhibition space, yet a challenging and multi-dimensional one.

Available: Spring 2010

Colophon

Published by
MuseumsEtc
8 Albany Street
Edinburgh EH1 3QB
www.museumsetc.com

ISBN: 978-0-9561943-3-6
British Library Cataloguing in Publication information available

Text: Underware Dolly, 10/15pt

Lightning Source UK Ltd.
Milton Keynes UK
13 March 2010

151324UK00001B/30/P